CHICAGO PUBLIC

K00714 06588

D0282602

HC
141
.F72
1987

Fraser, Peter.

Central American
economic handbook

$80.00

DATE		

DISCARD

© THE BAKER & TAYLOR CO.

CENTRAL AMERICAN
ECONOMIC HANDBOOK

CENTRAL AMERICAN
ECONOMIC HANDBOOK

EUROMONITOR PUBLICATIONS LIMITED
87–88 Turnmill Street, London EC1M 5QU

**CENTRAL AMERICAN
ECONOMIC HANDBOOK**
First edition 1987

Other titles in this series:

The African Economic Handbook
The Caribbean Economic Handbook
The Third World Economic Handbook
The East European Economic Handbook
The USSR Economic Handbook
The China Economic Handbook
The South American Economic Handbook
The Middle East Economic Handbook
The Asian Economic Handbook
The Pacific Basin: An Economic Handbook
West European Economic Handbook

Published by
Euromonitor Publications Limited
87–88 Turnmill Street
London EC1M 5QU

Telephone: 01-251 8024
Telex: 21120 MONREF G

Copyright © Euromonitor Publications Ltd, 1987

*All rights reserved. No part of this book may be reproduced or utilized in any way,
mechanical or electronic, including photocopying, recording, or by any information
storage or retrieval systems, without prior permission in writing from the publisher.*

British Library Cataloguing in Publication Data

Fraser, Peter D.
   Central American economic handbook.
   1. Central America —— Economic conditions ——1979-
   I. Title   II. Payne, Mark
   330.9728′053   HC141

   ISBN 0-86338-218-5

Typeset by Hands Fotoset, Leicester
Printed in Great Britain by St Edmundsbury Press, Bury St Edmunds, Suffolk.

FOREWORD

Political and financial instability have underpinned recent political and economic history in the seven countries which constitute the region known as Central America, a region which has consequently attracted considerable international interest—and mounting concern —over the last decade.

The region is dominated geographically and economically by Mexico and, in turn, by the United States itself. There are considerable disparities of wealth, and the widely differing political conditions have fostered considerable volatility in terms of recent economic development: it is a region living on the brink.

Whether Central America can resolve the major problems it currently faces and the potential impact on the world economy are among the major issues explored in *The Central American Economic Handbook*, a major new study in the Euromonitor series of regional economic studies. The handbook features ten chapters which identify and analyse both the economic progress and prospects of the Central-American region as a whole and the major developments within each of the countries within the region. The handbook features an in-depth profile of the Mexican economy, and a wealth of up-to-date factual data on socio-economic trends and developments. A statistical factfile of key economic parameters is appended.

The principal authors of *The Central American Economic Handbook* are Peter Fraser and Mark Payne.

Peter Fraser who wrote the overview chapters, is a writer and lecturer in Latin American affairs based at the Department of Historical and Cultural Studies at London University Goldsmiths' College. Mark Payne, who contributed the chapter on Mexico, is business writer and international market analyst with extensive knowledge of the Mexican economy. Other country sections were compiled by economic journalists.

CONTENTS

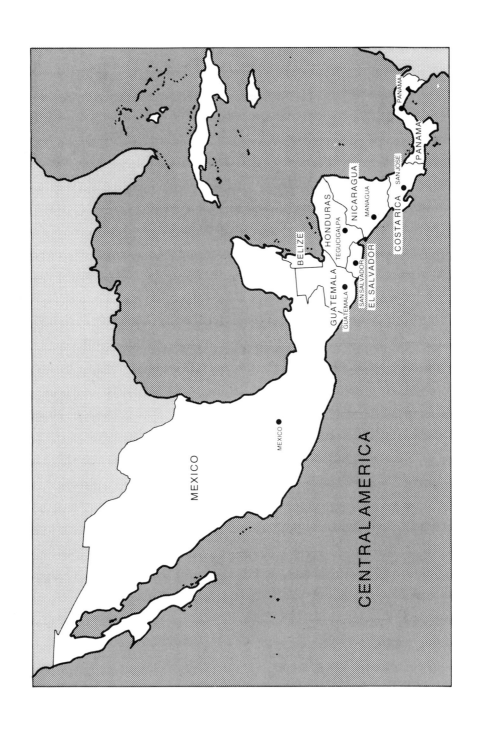

MEXICO

MEXICO

BELIZE

GUATEMALA
GUATEMALA

HONDURAS
TEGUCIGALPA

SAN SALVADOR
EL SALVADOR

NICARAGUA
MANAGUA

COSTA RICA
SAN JOSÉ

PANAMA
PANAMA

CENTRAL AMERICA

CHAPTER ONE
CENTRAL AMERICA IN A WORLD CONTEXT

I   The global perspective

Mexico and Central America have attracted unusual attention on the international scene in the eighties. Mexico's debts and the violence of recent Central-American political history have been major news items during this time, altering the image of a region best known for Mexican oil, the Panama Canal, and the bananas and coffee from the other countries. The significance of the debts and the violence reflects the enormous disparity in size, influence and power between Mexico and its southern neighbours: Mexican debts may endanger the world's banking system, and political turbulence of Central America has significance for some of the USA's political elite, although for few others than its victims.

For the states of Central America, including Mexico, the USA has long been the dominant power. For Mexico this has been so for nearly a century and a half, with the loss of its northern areas to the USA in the middle decades of the nineteenth century and for some decades into this century, with interventions and the threat of interventions. The only major European incursions were the French occupation at the time of the American Civil War and major British investments in the Mexican oil industry. For the other states American predomi-nance came in this century, though even during the British domination of the nineteenth century American interest and involvement could be decisive. After the failure of the French attempts to build a Panama Canal the Americans created Pana-manian independence to facilitate their own venture. The major economic developments of the late nineteenth and early twentieth centuries in the other small Central-American states—coffee and the bananas that earned them the scornful title 'banana republics'—were mainly under American control. The major problems facing Nicaragua in its international relations have nearly everything to do with its revolution changing that client relationship with the USA.

Historically, Mexico and Central America have not constituted a region. The Maya, Toltec and Aztec empires never controlled all the territory from Mexico to Panama; the Spaniards administered

Mexico, Panama and the other territories separately; Mexico and the states (except Panama) briefly united soon after independence; Panama, before its independence, was part of Colombia; and there was a short-lived Central American Federation in the 1820s and 1830s. The major divisions have therefore been (1) Mexico, (2) Honduras, Guatemala, El Salvador, Nicaragua, Costa Rica, and (3) Panama. More recently, Mexico has turned its attention towards the Caribbean and Central America, providing assistance during the oil crisis and playing a major role in the attempt to solve the region's problems peacefully, and Panama has wriggled a little way free from American domination and strengthened its links with its northern neighbours.

Culturally, these countries constitute part of Latin America, and Mexico and the Central-American countries have contributed many distinguished artists to the long list of famous Latin Americans in the twentieth century. Except for Costa Rica, all the countries belong to the sub-grouping of Latin-American states where the primary ethnic mixture is European and indigenous Indian, with Indian culture now of minor importance, except in Guatemala. The price of political participation has often been acquiring Spanish culture and losing the country's original culture. This was most brutally illustrated in El Salvador by the Matanza (massacre) of 1932 when a peasant rebellion by Indians resulted in 30,000 deaths and the virtual disappearance of Indian culture, as the remaining Indians shed their original cultural traits and assimilated Latin-American ones. Collective violence by some states, especially Guatemala, in recent years has contained a large element of keeping the Indians in their place. The revolutionary government in Nicaragua after 1979 was unable to avoid alienating sections of the Indian population, thus creating additional security problems for itself. Costa Rica, with its population of mainly European descent, and Mexico, with a revolution that widened political participation and increased acceptance of the original cultures, are the two countries with homogeneous cultures and minimal minority problems.

Since the Spanish Conquest, only Mexico and Panama have been of great importance to the world economy, interestingly for much the same reasons in the sixteenth as in the twentieth century. Mexico produced a large volume of silver for its Spanish conquerors, and its mineral resources, this time oil, have been of great importance since the beginning of the twentieth century. The importance of the Panama region in the sixteenth century was manifested by Panama

2

City being the original seat of Spanish government, extending south to Peru. It acquired this importance because it was at the thinnest part of the isthmus and thus became the trans-shipment point for treasure and goods between the Atlantic and Pacific territories of the Spaniards. In this century, with the building of the Panama Canal, it decisively overcame its nineteenth-century rival for such a canal, Nicaragua, and acquired strategic and economic significance out of all proportion to its size. The other countries were comparatively neglected parts of the Spanish Empire and only late in the nineteenth century became of any significance as producers of bananas and coffee. Panama, which until the late 1970s received rent from but did not control the Canal, became notorious for its being, with Liberia, one of the major flags of convenience for those ship-owners reluctant to fulfil the stringent registration requirements of the major maritime powers. More recently, generously framed banking laws have attracted large sums of money from dubious quarters.

All these countries have populations who live on the whole in poverty, though appreciably above levels available to people in many Asian and African countries, even in the three poorest countries: El Salvador, Honduras and Nicaragua. The enormous disparity in size between Mexico and the rest can immediately be seen by comparing the countries. Mexico has an area nearly four times, and a population more than three times, those of the others. In size and population, Mexico is one of the world's largest countries; the rest are small, exceeding in size only the mini- and micro-states which have achieved independence since the Second World War. Mexican national income in the mid 1980s made it the second largest economy of Latin America after Brazil, and its economy was larger than that of the Netherlands. Income per capita, however, was less than a quarter that of the Dutch, and roughly equal to the Panamanian level. Of the three Latin-American states (Argentina, Brazil and Mexico), Mexican income per capita is somewhat higher than Brazil's, but smaller than Argentina's. Mexico and Panama therefore have national per capita incomes roughly equal to Portugal, Malaysia and South Africa; Costa Rica and Guatemala have incomes approximating those of Mauritius and Turkey; and those of Nicaragua, El Salvador and Honduras are similar to those of Nigeria and Thailand. As export markets they are even smaller than these figures suggest, since incomes are very unequally distributed. Of these countries only Costa Rica, because of its advanced welfare facilities, has an infant mortality rate classified as low by the United Nations Children's Fund

(UNICEF); Panama is classified as medium (26 per 1000 compared to Costa Rica's 19); all the rest are classified as high, ranging from Mexico (55 per 1000) to Honduras (80). Despite the region's problems, these figures represent great improvements since the early 1960s. Unlike many other developing countries, literacy rates for men and women are approximately equal except in Guatemala, and over 80% of the population are literate in Costa Rica, Panama and Mexico. With their long tradition of higher education and high literacy rates, these countries have a much sounder basis for development than many countries with similar levels of income.

II Relations with the USA

Like most other countries since the Second World War, Mexico and Central America have been influenced in a number of ways by the United States of America. Their Latin culture and the use of Spanish have protected them to a certain extent from the influence of American culture, though fears of American cultural imperialism are strong among many members of the intelligentsia. Many elements of American culture have a strong appeal to the middle classes which have developed in this period, and the number of emigrants to the USA points to the wider appeal of that country. Religion also provides some measure of insulation, but in recent years there have been powerful and wealthy US evangelical Protestant missions operating in the region which have made powerful converts. General Efrain Rios Montt, who became President of Guatemala by means of a coup in 1982, is the best known of these converts. That his conversion had more than religious significance can be seen from his announcement soon after becoming President that he had received offers of millions of dollars from Protestant sects in the USA to develop a new political, economic and social order in Guatemala. Nothing came of it, but this proposal illustrates the fact that evangelical Protestantism has three aspects: a religious one, appealing very often to the marginalized minority groups excluded from participation in the Roman Catholic Church by the dominant groups; a cultural aspect, deriving from its North-American origins; and a political one, in that it is often a counter to the radicalization of the Roman Catholic clergy, especially those in the rural areas. Culture, religion and politics cannot therefore be easily separated in this region, and there is little indication that the powerful American forces wish to do so.

American influence has also been strong on the military forces of 'the region, except in Mexico and Costa Rica. This influence became particularly marked after the Cuban revolution. The example of a successful guerrilla war in Cuba inspired dissenters within many Latin-American countries to emulation and the Americans to fear successful imitations throughout Latin America, particularly in a region long regarded as America's back yard (the USA has a long history of intervention in the region). As mentioned above, in this century they intervened most notably in the creation of the Panamanian state by blocking the efforts of the Colombian troops to put down the rebellion; they attemped less successfully to intervene during the Mexican revolution, but had in the end to accept it, while being able to ensure that it was less radical than it might otherwise have been; they occupied Nicaragua from 1912 to 1933, paving the way for the Somoza dictatorship that directly or indirectly ruled Nicaragua from 1934 to 1979; and in 1954 they assisted in the overthrow of the Arbenz government in Guatemala because of its links with communists. US interventionism in the region up to the late 1940s was mainly to protect business interests in the region or, as during the Second World War, to depose dictators previously supported but then feared as threats to the strategically important Panama Canal because of their Nazi and fascist sympathies. From the late 1940s, with the beginning of the Cold War, the USA began to oppose actively all those in the region it recognized as communist, or who were regarded as communist by the political elites. This more ideological phase did not obliterate existing strategic or business interests; part of the opposition to the Arbenz government in Guatemala was caused by his attempts to control American banana interests.

A new phase of American involvement can be identified from the early 1960s. One lesson of the Cuban revolution was that attempts to overthrow unpopular governments (unpopular with the Americans and their political allies, more popular with the people) were likely to be less successful than in the past, and that prevention was better than cure. This led to the armed forces being given American training and equipment to make sure that they could defeat any insurgent movements. Nationally, in state after state, this strengthened the position of the military; internationally, it strengthened the position of the USA by creating cadres of American-trained officers dependent on the continued good-will of the USA for supplies of arms and material reward. It also had for the USA the unforeseen effect of reducing their influence on the military, an effect that became clear during the Carter administration. Carter's emphasis on human rights in Central America, as elsewhere, could not work in places like Guatemala and El Salvador for the simple reason that the military of those countries would not allow it to work. Having made the military the most powerful section in society, with power independent of the wealthy elites of those societies, the USA could not cease to support them without causing the collapse of the anti-communist forces. With the presidency of Reagan, human rights were either neglected or redefined in assessing the most embattled regimes which were also the most repressive, although cosmetic changes were made by having civilian presidents elected. These presidents possess very little power compared to their military chiefs, and the only truly civilian governments in the region are those of Costa Rica and Mexico, both of which significantly escaped the close attentions of the USA in the 1960s.

Relations with the USA can be illuminated by examining briefly the Caribbean Basin Initiative (CBI) and US responses to the Contadora and Costa Rican peace proposals. The Caribbean Basin Initiative which, as its name suggests, applied to the Caribbean islands as well, was hailed by some regional leaders with enthusiasm, some comparing it to the Marshall Plan for Europe in the post-war years. It is a mixture of aid and concessions to the region's exporters which has benefited some countries, most notably those that the USA considered most at risk. Thus, of the first $350 million, two-thirds went to El Salvador (receiving over a third), Costa Rica and Honduras. The first of these was under great pressure from guerrilla forces at that time, the second in a grave economic crisis, and the last the site of the massive American military build-up. One of the criteria for receiving aid was that a country was not communist, immediately eliminating Cuba and Nicaragua. When Mexico joined the CBI along with Canada and Venezuela, it repudiated any intention of fighting communism, but the CBI continues to be seen as a means of rewarding US allies identified as being at risk. It has proved of benefit to manufacturing in the region by keeping open US markets while protectionist sentiment and measures have been common. It is improbable, however, that the CBI will prove more effective in transforming Central-American economies and societies than the Alliance for Progress of the 1960s.

Both the Costa Rican and Contadora peace plans start from a premiss rejected by the USA: that the causes of instability in the region are seen as indigenous, not the result of communist subversion. Hence, both have classified US support for the anti-government forces in Nicaragua (the contras) as no different from any other foreign support of anti-government forces elsewhere in the region. The Contadora group comprises Mexico, Panama and the two South-American states bordering the Caribbean Sea—Colombia and Venezuela. Brazil also expressed support for its proposals. Despite the extent of such support from important Latin-American countries, the USA, while publicly expressing its own support, has privately declared that it will not allow it to interfere with US policy objectives. It has also encouraged its clients in the region, especially El Salvador and Honduras, to place obstacles in its way. Similar tactics have been used to subvert the Costa Rican proposals. For a period in the 1980s under the presidency of Luis Alberto Monge, Costa Rica, dependent on US aid to salvage its economy, became hawkish towards Nicaragua. A new policy was adopted in 1986 with Oscar Arias' accession to the presidency. His plan dealt with guerrilla movements throughout the region and moves towards greater democracy and freedom in both Nicaragua and El Salvador. At the end of 1986 the proposals seemed dead, with US opposition expressed openly and through El Salvador and Honduras. Arias' persistance paid off when, in August 1987, the presidents of Guatemala, El Salvador, Honduras, Nicaragua and Costa Rica met in Guatemala City and agreed to liberalization in Nicaragua and El Salvador. Despite these agreements, fears remain that the USA will once more put pressure on its staunchest allies, El Salvador and Honduras, to wreck the plan. At the time of writing, soon after the agreement, the US Government continues to speak and act ambiguously, and the success of the agreement will depend on the balance of forces within the Republican Party and between the President and Congress. Given US attitudes to proposals in the past which have not given it all that it wanted, the Guatemala City agreement has an uncertain future.

Relations with the USA, particularly in this century, have been shaped by the great disparity in the economic and military power between the USA and the states of the region, even the largest one, Mexico. This situation is unlikely to change, even if Reagan is replaced in the 1988 elections.

III Relations with South America

Relations with South America have not been strong. In the sphere of culture there has long been a very strong link among the Spanish-speaking nations of the Americas, but political relations have been troubled and economic links weak. The Organization of American States (OAS) has provided a means of linking these states together, but until recently was almost wholly dominated by the USA. Political relations within Latin America were often determined by political affinity, with the states with representative institutions under civilian rule having cool relations with the military authoritarian governments. Hence, the military regime in Argentina had good relations with Somoza's Nicaragua, and provided expertise to El Salvador in the early 1980s. The Contadora group included the two South-American states on the Caribbean, Colombia and Venezuela, and invited the Dominican Republic to their third meeting. Cuba has quite strong links with Nicaragua. Relations with Nicaragua have varied most markedly, depending on the complexion (and attitude to communism) of civilian governments. The unity of the Latin-American states remains cultural and rhetorical, rather than political.

Economic links with South America are equally weak. The one exception is Panama, with its entrepôt status. About 60% of its re-exports are to other Latin-American countries. All the others, including Mexico, export little to and import equally small amounts from South America. The US severing of relations with Nicaragua has already produced some change in its major trading partners, but these have not been South American (although Latin-American countries such as Brazil and Venezuela have supplied it with credits). Exports to and imports from these countries from South America usually comprise less than 5% of total trade.

There is, however, one major concordat between the region and South America: the San Jose agreements of 1980 and 1984. These agreements were made between Venezuela and Mexico on the one hand, and the Central-American states (including Panama) and some Caribbean states on the other. The oil producers promised to supply all the oil needs of these states at world market prices, but with 30% of the price to be remitted as loans. These loans, at low interest rates, were initially for five years, but if used for projects deemed to be of primary development importance, stretched to twenty years at even lower rates. The agreements were extended for another five years in 1984.

IV   Political instability

At a very general level, the causes of instability in this region are no different to those in other developing countries. Rising expectations and ready access, both by travel and the mass media, to high levels of consumption in rich countries, especially the USA, make people in poorer countries discontented with their living standards and impatient of governments unable to fulfil their expectations quickly. This has been fairly common since the early 1950s throughout the developing world, and Central America, so open to American influence and so close to the USA, cannot be an exception. There are, however, causes more specific to the region.

Mexico and the Central-American countries have a long tradition of post-independence political instability. Periods of great instability in the nineteenth and twentieth centuries have led to long periods of autocratic rule, such as that of Porfirio Diaz in Mexico in the late nineteenth and early twentieth centuries, or of the Somoza in Nicaragua from the 1930s to the late 1970s. If we compare periods of instability after the other great twentieth-century revolutions, the Russian and the Chinese, to that after the revolution in Mexico, we can obtain some measure of this instability. The Mexican revolution led to nearly three decades of political turbulence with competing political forces, whereas in little more than a decade after the Russian revolution and the Chinese one of 1949, state power was firmly in the hands of one party, and has remained so. In this respect, the Mexican revolution more closely resembles the earlier Chinese revolution of 1911, which resulted in four decades of instability. To a limited extent, a history of political instability does render future stability less likely, but an examination of the two most stable countries in the region, Mexico and Costa Rica, suggests the fundamental causes of this high degree of instability. Their most salient characteristics in this respect are their reforms, the absence of the military in politics, and political systems which, by keeping the extreme left and right in check, allow little opportunity for foreign intervention.

Since agriculture remains so important a sector in these economies, land reform has been one of the most pressing political issues in the region. For Mexico, the *ejido* system of land tenure which was developed after the revolution to replace the large *haciendas* provided the major reform; in Costa Rica, welfare reforms dating back to the early 1940s and a less inequitable distribution of wealth have ameliorated the conditions of the poorer people. Inequalities are very pronounced in the other countries. El Salvador has moved some way from the days of the '14 families', but in this, the most densely populated state in the region, about 65% of the rural population in 1980 was estimated to own no land. The programme of land reform announced in 1980 has had very litle effect on changing this situation, because of the opposition of major land-owners. In Guatemala, it was land reform that proved to be Arbenz's undoing in 1954 when he tried to split up the United Fruit Company's holdings by appropriating uncultivated land (the company claimed that only 20% of its land was uncultivated; its opponents said 85%). By the 1970s, some improvement had taken place: about 2% of the population owned slightly more than half the cultivable land, compared to over two-thirds three decades before. Even USAID concluded that Guatemala had the most uneven distribution of land in the region. In 1986 the Government declared their intention of establishing a land bank to provide easy credit for purchasing land, but the scheme would benefit less than 5% of the landless. Honduras launched its own land reform programme in 1961, but land redistribution was implemented with vigour only in the mid 1970s when Colonel Melgar Castro was head of government. In the 1980s it has been asserted that army officers rather than the landless have been the beneficiaries of reform, as in Guatemala. Nicaragua, since the revolution, although not until 1981, has begun an extensive programme of land redistribution which was speeded up in 1985 but has run into domestic opposition from large land-holders. The Panamanian economy's comparatively unimportant agricultural sector makes this an equally unimportant issue there. Landless peasants have formed an important sector of all guerrilla movements in the region, and indiscriminate military action against peasants has merely strengthened rural opposition to governments, in Nicaragua successfully, in El Salvador and Guatemala so far unsuccessfully, in a replay of the story of the Mexican revolution. The continued existence of small groups of rural oligarchs, despite recent industrial-izations and modernizations, goes a long way towards explaining persistent instability.

These conditions support, and are supported by, the military apparatuses of the region. In Mexico, civilians took some time after the revolution to assert their authority; as a consequence, Mexican military forces are small compared to those of its smaller southern neighbours, with the exception of Costa Rica. After its civil war of the 1940s, the army was abolished in Costa Rica and so far the National Guard has been kept small and in check, although there have been fears that the continuing tension in the region could lead to its size and power expanding. In all other countries, despite their ostensibly civilian governments, the military, whether the army or the National Guard, remain the real rulers of the country. This can be observed quite openly in their dominance in Honduras, and the limited room for manoeuvre of the El Salvador and Guatemala civilian presidents and, more recently, in July 1987 in Panama. In that country, fierce opposition to the commander of the Panamanian Defence Forces and the real ruler of the country, General Noreiga, came temporarily at least to a halt, despite strong support from the USA for middle-class demands that he should leave. The military, once the oligarchies' weapon to keep their labourers under control, has become an interest in its own right. At times, as with most military officers, it merely joins the elite; at others, for example under Colonel Castro in Guatemala and General Torrijos in Panama, it can act against the interests of the oligarchs. In exceptional circumstances, as with the first Somoza, a military officer can establish himself as the founder of the most powerful family of oligarchs, but the replication of Somoza's feat is now virtually impossible. However the military acts, its replacement by other than military means remains unlikely; hence the guerrilla movements.

Costa Rica and Mexico have a final characteristic that other countries lack: political systems which have kept political extremes in check. This was achieved in Costa Rica after the civil war of the 1940s, and in Mexico in the decades after the revolution. This characteristic has more to do with the likelihood of foreign intervention than with any intrinsic merit of such a system. If the system tilts too far to the right, as with Somoza's Nicaragua or Guatemala and El Salvador in the 1970s, support for guerrilla movements comes first from within the region; Costa Rica was important in supporting the anti-Somoza forces. It may also come from Cuba and the Eastern Bloc, though US fears of such intervention have often proved groundless. Alternatively, it may come from the USA, sometimes to achieve a more moderate government or remove the most reactionary figures (events in

Panama in July 1987 fall into this category) or, if anti-government forces seem particularly strong, to prop up faltering regimes. If the government, as in Guatemala under Arbenz or Nicaragua under the Sandinistas, is perceived by the USA to be too far to the left, it intervenes to replace it. In none of these circumstances can governments approximating those of Costa Rica or Mexico come to power, and the political system remains highly unstable.

By examining individual countries, we can assess the different degrees of stability and the most likely threats to their political systems. The most stable countries are Mexico and Costa Rica, but both face potential threats to stability from the austerity measures that have had to be adopted to cope with their massive debts. Costa Rica, in addition, has suffered from its involvement, voluntary and involuntary, in regional conflict. The next most stable countries are Panama and Honduras, for radically different reasons. Panama, with its high per capita income, benefits from its modernization; Honduras, if not its people, benefits from its lack of modernization and its low population density, which makes land reform a less explosive issue elsewhere. In Panama, a comparatively large middle class threatening the hegemony of the military poses the largest threat to stability; in Honduras, the massive American military expansion provides a potentially destabilizing force. Guatemala, with its successful campaign against guerrilla movements, has achieved some stability, but the causes of anti-government revolt have not been removed. The most unstable countries are El Salvador and Nicaragua. In El Salvador, massive military aid and little reform contribute to continuing instability. In Nicaragua, political mistakes and US assistance for anti-government forces destabilize the regime.

V Inter-country comparisons

In the decades after the Second World War, all the countries in the region grew quite strongly, but by the early 1970s signs of problems appeared. Costa Rican balance of payments problems led to tariffs against fellow CACM members being imposed, and the subsequent decay of the CACM. In the decade from the first oil price rise in 1973, economic performances began to vary widely.

From 1973 to 1983 two countries' economies actually shrank: those of Nicaragua and El Salvador. It was no coincidence that these were the countries most affected by internal strife. The economies that grew most strongly were those of Mexico, not surprisingly, and Panama. Mexican growth can be attributed to its being an oil producer; Panamanian growth to the expansion of its services, especially in the financial sector. If we examine per capita growth, Costa Rica joins the group that declines and Mexico cedes its first position to Panama. Guatemala and Honduras showed very small growth rates. A comparison of Gross Domestic Product in 1980 and 1985 (except for Guatemala) shows a decline for El Salvador, tiny expansion for Costa Rica, roughly equivalent expansion for Honduras and Nicaragua, and Mexico once more in second place to Panama. These figures confirm the effects of instability on El Salvador, but demonstrate the recovery of Nicaragua from the Somoza years and the continuing benefits that the Panamanian economy reaps from its international financial sector.

TABLE 1.1   GNP GROWTH RATES BY COUNTRY 1973–1983

Country	GNP real growth rate	GNP per capita real growth rate
Costa Rica	2.4	−0.1
El Salvador	−0.2	−3.0
Guatemala	3.7	0.7
Honduras	3.9	0.4
Mexico	5.0	2.0
Nicaragua	−1.3	−5.0
Panama	4.8	2.5

Source: World Bank

   Though agriculture has been declining in importance in recent decades, in every country except Mexico and Panama it still contributes over 20% of the Gross Domestic Product. In Nicaragua, Guatemala and Honduras it contributes more than a quarter, in El Salvador and Costa Rica about 20%, and in Mexico and Panama less than 10%. Agriculture's share of the labour force remains high, in no country being less than a quarter. Panama, Mexico and Costa Rica have the lowest shares with 25–27%, El Salvador and Nicaragua about 40%, while in Guatemala and Honduras over half the labour force is employed in agriculture. Manufacturing constitutes a larger sector of the economy in Mexico, Nicaragua and Costa Rica, being three times as large as agriculture in Mexico, approximately the same size in Nicaragua, and slightly larger in Costa Rica. Elsewhere it is a

smaller sector, with manufacturing in Honduras being less than half
the size of agriculture. In every country, however, it employs
significantly fewer people than agriculture, varying from about one-
fifth in Guatemala to about half in Costa Rica. The failure of
manufacturing to absorb labour while the agricultural labour force
has been declining constitutes one of the gravest problems of the
region, where urban populations have grown faster than the general
population.

TABLE 1.2   SHARES OF GDP AND EMPLOYMENT: AGRICULTURE AND
            MANUFACTURING

Country	Percentage of GDP[1]		Percentage of labour force[2]	
	Agriculture	Manufacturing	Agriculture	Manufacturing
Mexico	8.6	24.4	29.0	11.7
Panama	9.9	8.9	26.0	9.6
Costa Rica	20.0	22.0	31.4	13.3
El Salvador	20.8	15.8	40.0	n.a.
Nicaragua	25.0	25.0	40.0	18.0
Guatemala	25.5	15.6	53.6[3]	10.5[3]
Honduras	27.5	12.4	57.2	13.3

Source: IMF/national statistics/Euromonitor/ILO
Notes: [1] GDP statistics relate to 1985/6
       [2] Employment statistics relate to 1984
       [3] 1981 figures

The economic structure of Mexico and Panama differs markedly
from that of the other states. In the other countries agriculture
remains the dominant activity, while in Mexico and Panama the share
of agriculture in the economy is quite small. In Mexico, manufacturing and the oil industry are dominant; in Panama, international
services predominate. Manufacturing in the other countries shows
signs of healthy growth, and increasingly intermediate and capital
goods are taking a larger share of their imports. Agriculture,
however, and the predominance of a few items in export agriculture,
leave them in a much weaker position internally than Mexico and
Panama.

These differences are reflected in the balance of trade and balance
of payments figures. The early 1980s proved very difficult for all these
countries, but by 1982 Mexico had a surplus on its balance of trade
while of the others, only Costa Rica and Guatemala managed small
surpluses in two of the five years from 1982. By 1983, Mexico and
Panama had surpluses on their balance of payments, with the other

countries running high deficits. All this bears directly on the issue of debt repayments and does suggest the potentially very weak position of those countries, such as Costa Rica and El Salvador, which receive massive US economic assistance.

Of these countries, only Costa Rica (34.8%) and Panama (38.6%) have less than two-fifths of their population aged fourteen years or less, and almost half (47.7%) of the Honduran population falls into that category. Mexico, Panama and Costa Rica have the most literate populations with Honduras, Guatemala and Nicaragua having the least. Population growth for the period 1973–1985 has been lowest in Panama (2.3%), highest in Honduras (3.5%), with all the rest bunched together in the range 2.8–3.1%. These high growth rates constantly eat into the gains of economic growth and contribute to the expansion of urban populations with high levels of unemployment and poverty.

TABLE 1.3   URBAN POPULATION AND POPULATION GROWTH

Country	% Urban population 1983	Population growth rate (%) 1973–1985	Urban population growth rate (%)
Honduras	38	3.5	5.8
Guatemala	40	3.1	4.1
El Salvador	42	3.0	3.6
Costa Rica	45	2.4	3.2
Panama	51	2.3	3.0
Nicaragua	58	3.5	5.8
Mexico	69	2.4	3.2

Source: UNICEF

VI   International outlook

Unless there is a catastrophe in the Gulf, the price of oil is likely to remain low compared to the late 1970s and early 1980s. Without a recovery much stronger than currently forecast in world production, the demand for oil and its products will remain low. Low prices and weak demand offer no solution to Mexican problems in the immediate future. Its large population compared to the Middle-

Eastern oil states means that its oil revenues are much smaller comparatively, and like Nigeria, for instance, the current state of the oil market has much graver consequences than for Saudi Arabia, much less Kuwait. Because of its size as a debtor, creditors are likely to be more accommodating than to smaller debtors, and the new debt for equity arrangements may have very beneficial effects on Mexican enterprises by bringing in foreign expertise.

Oil prices, which are low for Mexico, remain high for other countries in the region, especially since the demand and prices for their own exports have been so low. Bananas, coffee, cotton, sugar and beef exports, as the other countries have discovered, are unlikely to provide strong recoveries, and the search for new exports, agricultural and industrial, and unconventional energy sources will have to continue. US interest in shoring up countries in the region deemed to be under threat with aid and through the Caribbean Basin Initiative will continue to postpone solutions to the most pressing economic and social problems. Europe has the opportunity, as it has shown to a certain extent with Nicaragua, to play a greater role in the region as aid donor and trading partner, though the role of Eastern Europe and the USSR will probably remain limited to assisting Nicaragua.

A major factor influencing foreign interest in the region will remain the political instability endemic to so many countries. The causes of the instability are internal, so that any successful effort will have to address itself to those causes and the vested interests which maintain them. This would be a preliminary to lifting these economies out of their poverty and providing the region with the domestic and foreign investment that it needs to develop.

CHAPTER TWO
REGIONAL INTERDEPENDENCE

I Political relations and defence

Political relations between these states have two main sources: those normal to inter-state relations, tradition, ideology and rivalry, whether economic or otherwise; and US influence, especially from the 1950s to the mid 1980s, although now seemingly less powerful in the late 1980s.

The largest state in the region, Mexico, has tended to deal more with the USA and South-American states than with those of Central America. Recent moves suggest that it will play a much larger role than formerly. The San Jose agreements of 1980 and 1984 show its growing interest in the Caribbean Basin; this trend receives further impetus from Mexican attention to its own southern areas bordering the Caribbean, and from the expansion of research on the Caribbean countries. Mexico's involvement in the Contadora process, despite US opposition, is also indicative of this search for a new role.

Panama, from the time of its creation, could not avoid closer links with the USA than with its neighbours. Post-war Panama has always been prone to bursts of anti-US feeling, though the Canal treaties are removing the major reason for this. Panama assisted the Sandinistas before their victory and subsequently, like Mexico, has been one of the sponsors of the Contadora process. Under General Torrijos, Panama generally favoured opposition to less radical governments in the region, but with his death the military, now facing internal opposition, may move closer to the other military-dominated Central-American regimes.

Costa Rica, in the unique position of being the only well-established democracy in the region, has always steered a difficult path in its relations with the other states and with the USA. At one time a member of the short-lived nineteenth-century federation, it was a member of the Central American Common Market, and its promotion of peace in the region also shows its commitment to better regional relations. Relations with the other states have been made difficult by its defence of democratic values, and this has proved especially troublesome in relations with Nicaragua. Under the

Somoza dynasty, Nicaragua often threatened Costa Rica, which, for reasons of self-defence as much as ideology, supported the anti-government forces. Relations with post-revolutionary Nicaragua were good for a while, but deteriorated sharply with the presence of anti-Nicaraguan factions in Costa Rica and became very strained under the presidency of Monge. The recent accord in August 1987, orchestrated by President Arias of Costa Rica, has been more in tune with Costa Rica's traditional role in the region of seeking peace and promoting democracy. Its economic fragility exposes it to US pressure, which was influential in the aggressive stance towards Nicaragua under Monge, although under Arias, confidence seems to have been restored.

Nicaragua has had the most volatile relations with the other states. Only Mexico has been consistent in its support for the revolutionary government, with Panama being generally supportive or, at the very least, neutral. With Costa Rica, relations as sketched out previously have been mixed. Relations with Guatemala have improved to the extent that Guatemala supported the Costa Rican peace plan. This was more the result of increased confidence among the military of Guatemala in their ability to keep guerrilla forces under control and distance from Nicaragua than any profound reassessment of the Nicaraguan revolution by the Guatemalans or changed policies by the Nicaraguans. With El Salvador and Honduras, relations deteriorated very quickly. In the case of El Salvador, Nicaragua supported anti-government guerrillas; Honduras contained bases for anti-Sandinista forces. Relations with these two countries have very little prospect of improvement unless anti-government forces arrive at accords with their respective governments.

El Salvador and Honduras, currently allies, have not always been so in the recent past. It was the infamous 'football war' of 1969 that led to the Central American Common Market sinking into decline. The conflict arose not out of any ideological disagreement (both governments were equally reactionary), but out of their differing population densities. Salvadoreans migrated to Honduras where they could find land; Honduran sensitivity on the issue was increased as they felt that other countries, especially El Salvador, were benefiting more from the CACM than themselves. At the moment, the two countries' dependence on the USA brings them together in an anti-Nicaraguan alliance.

Guatemala ideologically belongs to the same camp as El Salvador and Honduras, but has recently supported Costa Rican peace attempts. As explained above, part of the reason is their comparative success in suppressing guerrilla activity; and it is also as a result of the degree of independence they found they possessed when they successfully resisted US pressure in the late 1970s to improve their human rights record. This independence, in turn, partly derived from the fact that Guatemala had always maintained some distance from other countries' conflicts, despite US pressures, and more recently the civilian government has achieved some small measure of independence from the real rulers, the military. Guatemala's major source of tension is its claim on Belize. This brings it into potential conflict with the UK which stations troops and aircraft in this former British colony to deter, so far successfully, any Guatemalan invasion.

Since the failure of Cuban-inspired (and sometimes backed) revolutionary movements of the early 1960s, and the Cuban missile crisis of 1962, Cuban and Soviet threats to destabilize the region have receded, despite recent US attempts to exaggerate them. The defence of the region against external threats rests in the hands of the USA. Defence expenditure in the region tends to be heavily committed to combating internal dissent: Costa Rica devotes 3% of central government spending to defence, Mexico only 2.7%, while El Salvador spends 20% and Guatemala 25% (1985 figures). Mexico, it need hardly be added, is a much more tempting target for an aggressive enemy than either El Salvador or Guatemala. Costa Rica, recognizing the internally destabilizing effects of large military forces, has devoted its spending to more useful ends.

The US defence of the region is concentrated in Panama, where the US Southern Command deploys 100,000 military personnel on its fourteen bases. This concentration proceeds from the need to defend the strategically important Panama Canal, but also proves useful for the monitoring of regional conflict. In recent years, Honduras has also become the site of US bases, especially for training purposes, although there was opposition to this development in Panama, and the USA had to threaten the cutting off of aid to compel Hondurans to accept Salvadoreans for training in Honduras. The potential threat to the Canal comes from the USSR, but more for reasons to do with super-power rivalry elsewhere in the world than conflict between them in the region. Since the Cuban missile crisis the USSR has walked warily in the region, and the enormous strain that Cuba places on the Soviet economy suggests that further commitments will be made only reluctantly. Cuba itself poses a threat to the region more by example than by direct action, and does not possess the military strength to threaten regional security. In this light, joint US and Honduran manoeuvres appear to be intended to overawe the Nicaraguans and to allow the military to exercise, rather than to represent any immediate threat.

The threat to regional security is internal, and proceeds from internal causes. Here, at least, there has been evidence in the past of the co-operation of ideologically similar groups in their opposition to governments across the region, but the multiplicity of opposition groups prevents such co-operation from being uncontrollable for governments. Many influential US advisors think that the battle against the anti-government forces has been won, and that the US can adopt a less hysterical attitude to conflict in the region. Whether or not this happens, political relations in the region will remain volatile, and regional defence will rest not on co-operation by the states in the region but on US forces.

II   Employment and migration

The structure of employment in the region has been described in the previous chapter: the dependence on agriculture in most small countries, the small contribution of industry, and the effect of the austerity programmes of recent years in reducing the size of state employment. High rates of population increase have reduced the effects of high growth rates, and with the negative rates of the early 1980s have created problems of increasing unemployment in all countries. Table 2.1 shows the development of the problem.

TABLE 2.1   UNEMPLOYMENT AS A PERCENTAGE OF OFFICIAL
WORKFORCE 1980 AND 1985

Country	1980	1985
Costa Rica	8.0	11.5
El Salvador	15.0	33.0
Guatemala	15.0	19.0
Honduras	15.0	34.0
Mexico	8.0	18.5
Nicaragua	18.3	22.2
Panama	10.0	17.5

Source: National statistical agencies/Euromonitor

The economic performance of Costa Rica reflects the efficacy of US aid during those years rather than wonderful economic management; those of Honduras and El Salvador suggest that US military aid does little to the economy as a whole. In general, the figures show the effects of adverse international trends in commodity prices and of shrinking world trade on small open economies; the Mexican figures more than anything show the effects of falling oil prices and the debt crisis. Honduras, El Salvador and Mexico experienced a doubling in the rate of unemployment; in Guatemala and Nicaragua, rates rose by approximately 25%; Costa Rican unemployment rose slightly less than 50%, but from a low base; in Panama, rates rose by 75%, but once more from a low base. By 1985, therefore, Costa Rican unemployment was still the lowest in the region, but Mexico had overtaken Panama. The USA's two closest allies, Honduras and El Salvador, had done worst. Unofficial estimates from within the region tend to put unemployment and disguised unemployment much higher, but even the official statistics make gloomy reading, given the low levels of pay in the region.

Such rates of unemployment, and the political turmoil of the region, have led to high levels of emigration. Mexican emigration to the USA is the best documented, consisting of permanent legal migrants, illegal migrants and temporary workers. Between 1971 and 1984 nearly a million Mexican migrants were registered as being legally in the USA; in both 1983 and 1984 more than a million illegal Mexican migrants ('deportable aliens') were located in the USA. Migration from the Central-American countries to the USA is also high: between 1971 and 1984 slightly more than a quarter of a million people from Central America legally entered the USA. Of those, more than a quarter came from El Salvador, with Guatemala and Panama together supplying about one third. An estimate of Central Americans resident in the USA in 1979 put the number of Salvadoreans in the USA at 110,000, more than the number of Costa Ricans, Panamanians and Nicaraguans combined, and not far short of the combined total of Guatemalans (73,000) and Hondurans (53,000). This, of course, is the result of the high population density of El Salvador, even more than the result of political conflict. Conflict did have its effect, however, for some estimates suggest that half a million Salvadoreans were resident in the USA in 1982.

The USA has not been the only refuge for economic and political refugees. In 1978/9 about 110,000 Nicaraguans were living in neighbouring countries; in 1985 about 19,000 were in Honduras. In

1981 Salvadoreans were also moving to Central-American countries and Mexico: 173,500 were thought to be living there. 100,000 Guatemalans lived in Mexico in 1983. It has already been pointed out that even in days of comparative calm, the issue of Salvadorean migrants in Honduras could help to precipitate a war. In the 1980s large numbers of migrants and refugees impose great strains on the economies and politics of the host countries: economic austerity programmes exacerbate the effects of sudden accretions to the population; the political relations between states are worsened by the presence of politically motivated refugees. With unemployment rising in poor states such as these, the dislocations caused by additional mouths to feed and jobs to find are the last things the region needs.

III Inter-country trade

The major effort in the last three decades to expand inter-country trade has been the Central American Common Market (CACM). This was established in 1960 with Costa Rica, El Salvador, Guatemala, Honduras and Nicaragua being the signatories. By 1966 it had almost achieved intra-regional free trade and a common external tariff. But by the late 1960s, the uneven development of industrialization it had brought about began to lead to its disintegration. The war between Honduras and El Salvador helped the process of disintegration when Honduras withdrew in 1970, stating that it had nothing to gain from the CACM. Its achievements should not be underestimated, however: in 1961 intra-regional trade accounted for only 7.5% of these countries' trade, but had reached 25% in 1980 before declining to 16% in 1981. The CACM has clearly strengthened intra-regional trade, even if it has fallen short of expectations. In 1983 and 1984 the countries met to attempt to arrest this decline by providing preferential treatment among Central-American states on debt repayments, a common strategy to protect their balance of payments and various trade agreements.

Mexico and Panama have traditionally traded little with the CACM members, and though this may change in the future, at least with Mexico, Table 2.2 shows the differences between these countries very clearly.

TABLE 2.2   EXPORTS TO OTHER CENTRAL-AMERICAN COUNTRIES
AND MEXICO AS A PERCENTAGE OF EXPORT TRADE 1985

Country	% of exports
Guatemala	32
Costa Rica	24
El Salvador	21
Nicaragua	12
Honduras	6
Mexico	2
Panama	1

Source: derived from IMF tables

The only country that exported much to Mexico and Panama was Costa Rica, with US$49.9m, or just over a fifth of its regional trade. Guatemala and Honduras exported about 6–7% of their regional exports to Panama and Mexico, while the figure for Nicaragua and El Salvador was only about 3%. Mexico and Panama export an even smaller percentage of their total exports to the CACM countries.

A similar table of imports shows once again how little trade Mexico has with the other states, although it imports almost twice as much in total value as the other countries combined. The Panamanian figures, which show a sevenfold increase compared to its export figures, are explained by five-sevenths being imported from Mexico.

TABLE 2.3   IMPORTS FROM CENTRAL-AMERICAN COUNTRIES
AND MEXICO AS A PERCENTAGE OF IMPORTS 1985

Country	% of imports
El Salvador	30
Guatemala	28
Nicaragua	17
Honduras	16
Costa Rica	14
Panama	7
Mexico	0.2

Source: derived from IMF tables

A comparison of the two tables shows clearly the reasons for Honduran discontent: it imports almost three times as much in percentage terms as it exports to the rest of the region (by value: US$153.1m imports, US$51.6m exports). Costa Rica and Guatemala run surpluses; Nicaragua and El Salvador run substantial deficits on intra-regional trade, as does Panama (its deficit is mainly with Mexico). Mexico runs the largest surplus of all, although its total value is marginal in the context of the Mexican economy as a whole.

The chief beneficiaries of intra-regional trade are thus Costa Rica and Guatemala; the chief losers are El Salvador, Honduras and Nicaragua. Mexico benefits, but not in a significant fashion, and Panama, an apparent loser, depends more on its invisible exports for its balance of payments. All this is the result of uneven development, traditional trade structures and current political problems in the region.

IV   Debt flows

The region's debts are large, and have affected the economies of all countries. In attempting to deal with them, consumption has been cut and unemployment risen throughout the region. In the smaller states, foreign borrowing seemed a less painful alternative to higher taxation for the elites; in Mexico, the euphoria of the oil booms led to unwise borrowing. The differing abilities of countries to cope with their debt burdens have a strong political component: Mexico owes so much that its hand is strengthened; Costa Rica was regarded in the early 1980s as so important to US policies in the region that the USA provided massive assistance.

TABLE 2.4   RATIO OF FOREIGN DEBT TO FOREIGN RESERVES AND TO EXPORTS 1985

Country	Debt/reserves	Debt/exports
Honduras	25:1	3:1
Mexico	20:1	4.5:1
Nicaragua	14:1	19:1
El Salvador	13:1	2:1
Costa Rica	8:1	4.5:1
Guatemala	6:1	2.5:1
Panama	4:1	2:1

Source: IMF/Euromonitor/World Bank

Table 2.4 provides some idea of the size of the debt. The position of Honduras is much better than the table suggests: its debts were contracted at concessionary rates and its interest payments

(US$279m) in 1985 were low compared to those of other countries. Even so, it was forced to begin talks on rescheduling, which proved difficult since the government had not reached agreement with the IMF. The plight of Nicaragua shows up clearly: it had in 1985 neither sufficiently high levels of reserves nor export earnings for the size of its debt. In August 1987 it was encountering severe problems in trying to obtain enough oil for its needs.

Mexico stands alone in the magnitude of its problem. In 1986 interest and amortization of its US$74 billion debt amounted to US$10.91 billion, roughly two-thirds the value of its merchandise exports. Major debt restructuring programmes were implemented in 1986, and the move by some US banks to make provisions for bad debts to Third World countries (seven of them were owed US$13 billion by Mexico alone) may begin to tackle the problem. Another expedient that has been tried is the equity for debt swaps, in which foreign debtors aquire shares in Mexican companies. These amounted to over a billion US dollars in 1986 and almost half a billion in the first quarter of 1987. It is clear that there is no easy solution to the Mexican debt problem, and over the whole issue hangs the possibility that the bigger debtors, like Mexico, will co-operate in repudiating their debts.

V Foreign investment

The USA is the largest foreign investor in the region, having an estimated share of about two-thirds. In 1970 the USA invested nearly three times as much in Mexico as in the CACM countries, and twice as much in Panama as in the other five small states. These ratios have not altered very much; the highly diversified Mexican economy and the predominance of international financial services in that of Panama offer a much wider and more profitable field to the CACM economies. However, the development of the CACM countries has made them more attractive than before: in 1967 they attracted only 1.8% of direct foreign investment in Latin-American manufacturing, but by 1976 this had risen to 2.3%. The share of direct foreign investment which went into manufacturing also rose, from 19% of total investment in 1967 to 36% in 1976.

Foreign investment is particularly heavy in Mexican manufacturing, especially the automobile industry which makes engines for

European-manufactured cars. The Germans have invested heavily in steel, chemicals, fibres and pharmaceuticals; the Japanese in ships, steel and textiles. In Guatemala, the largest of foreign-owned companies was, perhaps not surprisingly, the Coca-Cola bottling plant, Embotelladora Guatemalteca SA, which the parent company took direct control over after industrial relations problems in 1980. After further troubles in 1985, the plant was taken over under franchise by Guatemalan investors and renamed Embotelladora Central. Being a foreign investor in the region, even in the more conservative countries, has not always proved easy.

In the early 1980s capital inflows began to contract sharply. With debt problems and servicing of loans, there now exists a net outflow of capital. From 1973 to 1981 net capital inflows into the CACM countries were equal to about 16% of the value of exports. From 1979 onwards they began to diminish. This had two main root causes: the behaviour of the banks, and the flight of capital from Latin America generally and the region in particular. Private capital, both foreign and domestic, became worried about the economic policies being pursued and fearful of the political turmoil in the region, and shifted their money out. This flight from Mexico, mainly for economic rather than political reasons, was exacerbated by the lack of any exchange controls. Foreign investment (equivalent to US investment) remains high in Honduras, which maintains a dominance in agriculture, but also controls the financial sector. Guatemala, also once dominated by US capital, has been going against the trend of falling foreign investment in the 1980s by attracting companies to its fledgling petroleum industry. The short-term economic and political prospects of the region are not likely to attract foreign investment in the quantities needed for development.

VI   Regional outlook

Except for the San Jose agreements when Mexico and Venezuela agreed to supply concessionary terms for oil purchases, and the attempts in 1983 and 1984 of the CACM states to co-ordinate economic policies, the current recession in world trade and the debt crisis have not strengthened regional bonds to any significant extent. In the future it is unlikely that Panama will become more involved in the regional economy, but Mexico may if its debt problems allow it to play a more significant role. The prospects for regional co-operation seem to lie mainly in the hands of the original CACM members.

A revival of the CACM seems, however, to be a distant prospect. The unevenness of economic development which wrecked the original attempt remains; political differences now exacerbate the original tensions. Nicaragua in the 1980s has been forced out of the US orbit and now trades extensively with Western and Eastern Europe rather than the USA, although a political settlement may lead to a revival of US trade with Nicaragua.

The chief economic problems of the region—debt and the devastation of political conflict—cannot be solved from within the region. The foreign debts of these states have to be settled in an international framework: a point abundantly clear in the Mexican case. Regional efforts, if backed by the USA, may achieve peace in the region, but the economic reconstruction of El Salvador and Nicaragua after the destruction of civil wars will have to find international solutions. In a region of open economies, the problem of low commodity prices and poor markets for manufacturing exports cannot be solved by regional means either. Since the economies of the region are not integrated, external events will continue to hinder any moves towards regional integration: a rise in oil prices, beneficial chiefly to Mexico, Guatemala as a small producer, and Panama, as refiner, adversely affect the others without much compensation; low oil prices, which affect the Mexican economy severely, benefit the others. The region's countries are likely to remain more linked with the major industrial economies than with each other.

CHAPTER THREE
MEXICO

I Introduction

Mexico is Latin America's second largest economy and boasts the region's second most substantial population. The country has made great strides forward since the 1960s, although since late 1982 it has been plagued by its massive level of external debt and by the collapse in the world oil price.

Los Estados Unidos Mexicanos together cover more than 10% of the land area of Latin America, of which the country is an integral part, and a substantial proportion of the North-American continent in which, strictly speaking, Mexico is located. This has in part led to a schizophrenic attitude on the part of Mexican officialdom over the decades, which sees the country as North American rather than Central or South American, and yet thoroughly Latin as far as relations with the United States are concerned.

Mexico is blessed with abundant natural resources, which, however, in one striking respect (the country's over-reliance earlier this decade on oil) could be held partly responsible for the economic plight in which the country now finds itself, and which will hamper development efforts at least until the end of the century. The country is not only a major oil producer, but also has become a significant gas producer, as well as an important source of silver, molybdenum, lead, zinc and copper, and a major industrial power within the developing world.

The country has been perhaps the most stable in Latin America since the early 1920s, a situation which has owed much to the autocratic nature of what has become effectively a one-party state, to the absence of a significant military corps and to the emergence of a very substantial middle class. While some observers feel that the national consensus which has existed/been imposed for the past sixty years and more is now in danger of disintegration under the weight of the country's economic problems, this is by no means certain. What is clear, however, is that the ability of Mexico's established political system to cope with current economic and social pressures for change will be tested to the full.

II Mexico's political system

Mexico remains one of Latin America's last non-democracies, despite its outward pretensions to be a democratic state. Nevertheless, the system which governs the country has overseen more than half a century of internal peace and almost as long a period of economic progress—the troubles of 1982/3 and 1986 notwithstanding. Furthermore, it is the system itself which acts as dictator, not the President of the Republic who, under the terms of Mexico's constitution, enjoys power for only a six-year term, after which he must step aside. Successors are chosen by outgoing presidents in order to attempt to achieve some form of policy continuity, after secretive discussions with the 'eminences grises' of the ruling party.

Mexico is governed—as it has been for decades—by the Partido Revolucionario Institucional (PRI) which, in theory, must contend in a free contest all elections to the presidency, governorships, Senate and Chamber of Deputies and local authorities. In practice the PRI tolerates no serious opposition and is not above electoral fraud—as is widely held to have been the case in the 1985 gubernatorial elections. While the great majority of Mexicans undoubtedly actually do support the PRI and its objectives in any event, such profound intolerance of genuine opposition is attracting increasing criticism within Mexico itself. The PRI itself operates by co-option of all important sectors of Mexican society; the corporate states trade unions (the 87-year-old leader of the country's leading trades union federation, Fidel Velasquez, has for decades been one of Mexico's powers behind the throne), the peasantry and white-collar workers are all integrated into the system, which oversees and widely distributes patronage at all levels of society (even the leader of the scavengers on the capital's appalling garbage dumps has been made a PRI deputy). In the 1982 presidential elections, Miguel de la Madrid (the current President) received 74% of the vote, compared to only 16% for his nearest rival from the increasingly vociferous Partido de Accion Nacional (PAN). With a natural edge like that, electoral fraud in 1985 suggests that tolerance of opposition parties (communism is almost unknown and certainly not accepted, despite Mexico's links with Cuba and incessant criticisms of the United States) runs only skin deep. The recent intolerance with which the radical views of Cuahautemoc Cardenas and the *corriente democratica* were met by the PRI amply illustrates this point.

In 1982 the corrupt and populist President Lopez Portillo was succeeded by his chosen successor, his former planning minister Miguel de la Madrid. The new President inherited the accumulated structural problems built into the Mexican economy under Portillo and his own predecessor Echevarria. Nominally anti-corruptionist, de la Madrid has launched the much-vaunted policy of 'moral renovation' which has concentrated its efforts on the prosecution of several key former corrupt officials (such as Diaz Serrano, head of PEMEX under the last administration). The former President, however, arguably the most personally corrupt individual in recent Mexican history, is regarded as untouchable, such is the awe in which the institution of the presidency itself is held. Furthermore, the anti-corruption campaign has not pressed too deeply into the Mexican system of graft and 'la mordita' ('the bite'), which is itself at bottom considered inviolate—and even a necessary evil.

In September 1987 de la Madrid named as his chosen successor the 39 year old planning minister Carlos Salinas de Gortari. A low-profile technocrat in the President's own former job, Salinas de Gortari has made something of a reputation for dealing with foreign bankers and will most probably ensure a policy continuity with the incumbent administration.

III   Demography

The population of Mexico has expanded rapidly in recent decades—indeed, alarmingly so from the point of view of the politicians and national economic planners faced with the task of trying to provide enough employment (to say nothing of nutrition, medical, educational and other services) in a period of economic crisis. Despite its official Catholic faith, birth control is widely encouraged by the state, even if it is not fully practised by the poorer and most fecund sectors of Mexican society. Indeed, only 40% of the women of child-bearing age actually use any form of contraception. In the 1984 national census the population totalled 76.8 million, and has increased at an annual average rate of 2.9% since 1973. Each year, almost two million more Mexicans are added to the national total, with the population exceeding 80 million by the start of 1987. By the end of the century it is widely expected that the population will greatly exceed 100 million.

The national birth rate during the first half of the 1980s has fluctuated around the 33–35 per thousand level—the second highest of all Latin-American countries—while the relative population increase has been exceeded only by that of Venezuela. The age structure of the national demographic profile also has worrying implications for Mexico's planners—well over 40% of the population are aged under 15, with child-bearing initiated at an early age by a majority of girls. In the long term, the health of Mexicans has exhibited marked improvements, although the recession which has gripped the country since late 1982 has cast some doubt on whether progress in this respect has been sustained most recently. Nutritional standards have also improved in the long term, with severe malnutrition relatively rare in Mexico. Life expectancy at birth in 1983/4 was 64 years for men and 68 years for women—up considerably from the 58 years and 61 years respectively which obtained in the mid 1960s. The mortality rate for infants has correspondingly declined, to a still high 5% in 1983/4 from over 8% in the mid 1960s. Educational standards, allied to the rising importance of Mexico's very large middle class, have also grown significantly, with more than half of children receiving at least secondary school education in the mid 1980s (while under one-fifth did so two decades earlier). The population density of Mexico as a whole is 41 persons per square kilometre—and rising—with a strong concentration in the high montane basin of Mexico. Founded by Hernan Cortes on the site of Montezuma's city of Technochtitlan, the national capital alone is host to over 20 million of Mexico's population—with some horrific projections suggesting that, by the turn of the century, what is already the world's largest agglomeration of human beings could boast up to 40 million inhabitants. Already the city is intolerably overcrowded, with millions of Mexicans living in lawless slums and shanty towns on the outskirts of Distrito Federal, with deprivation worsened by the effects of the 1985 earthquake. A permanent pall of pollution hangs over the capital, with automobiles and industry alike pouring noxious gases almost unchecked into the atmosphere to collect in a massive grey cloud. By the end of the century, life could become intolerable, with many scientists predicting that by 2010–2020 Mexico City will be physiologically uninhabitable. Quite apart from the overall social and economic crisis facing Mexico, the problems of the capital alone are etched deep into the psyche of politicians and bureaucrats alike—together the country's decision-makers—and will influence many national policy decisions between now and the end of the century.

The country contains a further 11 urban areas with populations in excess of approximately half a million. Mexico's second city is Guadalajara, with more than three million inhabitants, and its third is Monterrey, with 2.7 million inhabitants in 1984. Puebla de Zaragoza contains 1.2 million citizens, and Leon around 900,000. Sixth urban area is Ciudad Juarez with 750,000 inhabitants, and seventh is Tijuana, with a population in excess of 650,000. Torreon, Tampico, San Luis Potosi, Chihuahua and Veracruz all contain at least half a million people.

Overall, more than 70% of Mexico's population is urban, a proportion which has risen over the past two or three decades. The 'shift to the cities' has characterized all Latin-American countries, with the poor state of employment and services in the countryside inducing migration to towns of millions of Mexicans seeking (often in vain) a better life. The same pressures have underpinned the pressures for the migration of poor Mexicans to badly-paid and illegal jobs in the United States.

Unemployment is high in Mexico, and rose sharply during the economic recession of 1986. With an official national labour force of some 20 million (in a population of around 80 million), unofficial employment, as well as official underemployment and unemployment, is colossal. The official recognized rate of unemployment is modest indeed, fluctuating around 4–5% of the officially recognized labour force. In reality, it is in excess of 20%. Of total official employment, around one-quarter of persons are employed in agriculture, forestry or fishing, 13–14% in wholesaling, retailing, catering or the hotel sector, 12–13% in manufacturing industry, and over 30% in community, social and personal services. On balance, however, official figures are almost meaningless in attempting to understand the true nature of employment, underemployment, unemployment and poverty—the number of illegal immigrants crossing into the United States over the Rio Grande alone readily underlines this point. Furthermore, population growth of almost 3% per annum places further pressures on the labour system with each year that passes.

TABLE 3.1   RATES OF OPEN UNEMPLOYMENT IN URBAN AREAS
1985–1986

	1985				1986			
	Q1	Q2	Q3	Q4	Q1	Q2	Q3	Q4
All urban areas	5.2	3.9	4.6	3.7	4.1	3.8	4.9	4.3
Mexico City	5.7	4.3	5.2	4.4	4.9	4.4	5.8	5.1
Guadalajara	3.9	3.5	3.9	2.4	2.6	2.6	4.2	3.4
Monterrey	6.9	5.1	5.4	4.0	5.0	4.8	6.0	5.6

Source: Instituto Mexicano del Seguro Social/Instituto Nacional de Estadística,
Geografía y Informática

IV   The land

Mexico covers an area of 1,959,038 square kilometres, much of which
is inhospitable mountainous, desert or jungly terrain. Fully 29% of
the national land area is forested, and under one-fifth suitable for
agricultural cultivation—although livestock can be reared or ranched
on almost half of the national territory. Much of the country is higher
than 1000 metres, with an extremely wide range of climatic/
vegetational zones experienced moving both from north to south and
from sea level to the permanent snow caps of volcanoes such as
Popocatepetl and Orizaba. Apart from the jungle regions of the
tropical south, much of Mexico is arid or semi-arid, with irrigation
techniques necessary for the cultivation of many crops in most
regions of the country.

The central area of the Mexican Massif is formed of a complex
series of geological faults, basins and mountain ranges, although
basically the chain of central plateaux which runs south from the
Arizona-Texas frontier is flanked by the Sierra Madre Occidental in
the west and by the Sierra Madre Oriental in the east. The
intermontane basins ascend in altitude in a southerly direction, so
that the basin of Mexico itself, in which the capital district and the
world's largest urban agglomeration are located, is some 2300 metres
above sea level. South of the intermontane basins, the Mexican
Massif falls away gradually to the low-lying and hot Isthmus of
Tehuantepec, beyond which the terrain again rises to the highlands of
Chiapas, which are contiguous with Guatemala. North of Chiapas

lies the flat, low-lying and very hot Yucatan Peninsula, which comprises virtually the only extensive lowland in Mexico—although intermittently along the east and west coasts, particularly around Tampico and Los Mochis respectively, are fertile agricultural flatlands. The only other important region of Mexico, and almost totally isolated from the central Massif, is Baja California, which is in effect the southward extension of the Pacific coastal ranges of California.

V The Mexican economy

During the 1960s the Mexican economy grew by an average of almost 7% per annum under Presidents Lopez Mateos and Diaz Orduz, with a general policy of sound money pursual. Inflation rates were modest, indebtedness kept low, and balance of payments deficits never exceeded 3% of GDP. The situation changed, however, with the two populist administrations of Echeverria and Lopez Portillo and the borrow-spend policies of the 1970s. While economic expansion continued to run at an annual average of 6% under Echeverria and Portillo, expansionary policies coincided with several international recessions and reduced opportunities for Mexican non-oil exports. Inflationary pressures, balance of payments deficits, and high government and private sector borrowing ensued, while the policy of maintaining a grossly overvalued peso led to massive flights of capital from Mexico (often part of those same borrowings, in fact!). By the collapse of late 1982, the scene was set for economic disaster—at the end of that year the incoming de la Madrid administration was faced with foreign exchange reserves sufficient to cover only three weeks of imports, while interest payments on long-term debt amounted to almost one-fifth of the value of all Mexican exports. Furthermore, rapid population growth meant—and still means—that Mexico during the 1980s would have had to generate real growth of around 7.5% per annum merely to stand still in terms of job creation.

Table 3.2 amply illustrates the economic plight of Mexico during the late 1980s. In nominal pesos, Mexico's GDP rose from 45.6 billion in 1985 to a provisional 78 billion during 1986—which, however, represented a real decline of around 4%. Over 1980–6, as a whole the Mexican economy grew by no more than 4%, with a sharp reversal in late 1982–3 as the debt crisis struck, and again in 1986 (after several years of recovery) due to the plunging oil price. In per capita terms, however, it is clear that during the 1980s Mexico has been facing a crisis of the first order. Over 1980–6 per capita income, as measured by real prices, fell by fully 22% as the population continued to expand rapidly during a period of overall economic stagnation and of sharp cuts in public expenditure and private consumption. In 1986 per capita income averaged around US$1590— not desperately low at all by the standards of many other developing countries, but well down on the US$2290 of pre-recessionary 1982.

TABLE 3.2   EVOLUTION OF GROSS DOMESTIC PRODUCT 1980–1986

	1980	1981	1982	1983	1984	1985	1986p
Nominal value (bn pesos)	4.3	5.9	9.4	17.1	28.7	45.6	77.8
Constant 1980 value	4.3	4.6	4.6	4.3	4.5	4.6	4.4
% real growth	8.3	7.9	−0.6	−5.3	3.5	2.7	−4.0
Per capita nominal value ('000 pesos)	62	82	129	229	374	581	970
Per capita constant 1980 value	62	65	63	58	59	54	49
% real growth	5.4	5.1	−3.1	−7.6	1.5	−8.5	−9.3

Source: IMF/Banco de Mexico
Note: p – preliminary

By far the most important component of Mexican GDP is— interestingly, in view of the country's heavy reliance on crude oil sales for foreign exchange—the manufacturing sector of the country. It also proved relatively resilient during the 1986 national economic slump, accounting in that year for more of total GDP than in each of 1984 and 1985. Second component of the national economy is the wholesale, retail, catering and hotel sector—which again was relatively resilient during 1986. Traditionally the third component of Mexican GDP, the mining/petroleum extraction sector suffered a sharp real contraction in 1986, which enabled agriculture, fishing and forestry to move into third place.

Private consumption accounts for almost two-thirds of total expenditure on Mexican GDP, with public expenditure contributing a surprisingly modest 10%. Fixed investment (until 1986, at least!) is also a substantial contributory sector, as are exports (again, until 1986).

TABLE 3.3   COMPONENTS OF GDP 1984–1986

| | Pesos billion, current | | | % of total | | |
	1984	1985	1986	1984	1985	1986
Agriculture, livestock, forestry and fishing	2479	4091	7015	8.6	9.0	9.0
Mining (including petroleum)	2889	4145	5571	10.0	9.1	7.2
Manufacturing industry[1]	6857	11203	19852	23.8	24.7	25.5
Construction	1433	2299	3692	5.0	5.1	4.7
Electricity	277	419	912	1.0	0.9	1.2
Commerce, restaurants and hotels	6549	10533	18500	22.8	23.2	23.8
Transport and communications	2003	2975	5658	7.0	6.5	7.3
Financial services, insurance and real estate	1892	3089	5395	6.6	6.8	6.9
Other services	4723	6667	11182	16.4	14.7	14.4
TOTAL	28749[2]	45420	77778	100.0[2]	100.0	100.0

Source: Secretaría de Programación y Presupuesto/Banco de Mexico
Notes: [1] includes refined petroleum and petroleum products
[2] totals as published by Banco de Mexico do not sum exactly

TABLE 3.4   EXPENDITURE ON GDP 1985

(% of total)	
Private consumption	66.4
Government consumption	10.0
Fixed investment	16.9
Stockbuilding	2.3
Exports	12.2
Imports	−7.8
TOTAL	100.0

Source: IMF

VI   Government finance and expenditure

According to the Banco de Mexico, in 1985 the involvement of the public sector in the Mexican economy—as measured by government expenditure—amounted to 21.5%. This level was extremely low by the standards of OECD countries, and reflects the relatively modest level of welfare spending and defence activities engaged in by Mexico. Noticeably the PSBR in pre-recessionary 1981/2 was very high in relation to GDP, as the Lopez Portillo administration borrowed and spent as though the availability of international funds was limitless. In 1983–5 the PSBR was forced down to more manageable levels after the debt crisis struck and Mexico was forced into difficult negotiations with the IMF and foreign commercial banks. The PSBR is still, however, uncomfortably high, and rose sharply again during 1986 to an almost intolerable 16% plus of national GDP. Nevertheless, considering the magnitude of the revenue loss to the government of the 1986 shock (estimated at around US$7 billion in relation to programmed revenues), the fiscal weakening was far less than it would otherwise have been, owing to the adoption of substantial additional adjustment measures. Indeed, if interest payments are excluded from the equation, government finances were neatly balanced.

The economic deficit of the federal government and public sector enterprises and agencies, which accounts for the bulk of the PSBR, in 1986 reached 11.8 trillion pesos, an increase from 8.4% to 15.2% of GDP. The PSBR in total—the sum of the economic deficit and financial intermediation—increased to a record 12.7 trillion pesos.

TABLE 3.5   THE PSBR DEFICITS 1982–1986

(% of GDP)	1982	1983	1984	1985	1986p
PSBR	17.7	8.9	8.7	10.0	16.3
Economic deficit	16.3	8.3	7.3	8.4	15.2
Operational deficit	5.2	1.9	0.6	—	1.7
Primary balance	7.6	−4.4	−5.0	−3.7	−1.6

Source: Banco de Mexico
Note: p – provisional

Total expenditure by the Mexican public sector in 1986 reached a record 35.3 trillion pesos—or some 45.4% GDP. The ratio was sharply up on the 40.7% of 1985 due to the contraction in the actual level of GDP—although as a proportion overall during the 1980s, public expenditure has remained at or near the 45% level. Accordingly, in real terms, the virtual economic stagnation which has affected Mexico since late 1982 has not in fact substantially trimmed government spending as measured in relation to GDP. However, if

TABLE 3.6   THE PSBR 1982–1986

(% of GDP)	1982	1983	1984	1985	1986p
Economic deficit	16.3	8.3	7.3	8.4	15.2
– Budgetary sector	14.7	7.6	6.7	7.5	13.6
– Federal government	12.4	8.3	7.4	7.9	13.3
– PEMEX	1.4	−1.9	−1.7	−0.9	0.0
– Other	0.8	0.2	1.0	0.5	0.3
Off-budget enterprises and federal district departments	1.6	0.7	0.6	0.9	1.6
Requirements of development banks and trust funds	1.4	0.6	1.4	1.6	1.1
OVERALL PSBR	17.6	8.9	8.7	10.0	16.3

Source: Banco de Mexico
Note: p – provisional

the interest payment component of expenditure is taken out of calculations, in 1986 only 28.7% of total GDP was represented by public expenditure per se—down considerably from the 37.8% of pre-recessionary 1982. Capital spending by the public sector—again in relative terms—has further been halved over 1982–6 under the new-found financial stringency. During 1986, investment on public works suffered a reduction equivalent to 0.2% of GDP, while capital transfers increased by a corresponding amount.

On the revenue side of the public sector financial equation, government income in 1986 was only very marginally higher as a proportion of GDP than in 1982, and dipped sharply from the levels of 1983/4, due primarily to the reduction in the price of oil of 1986. Revenues from PEMEX collapsed, while the tax take in GDP terms rose substantially in 1986. In that year total public sector receipts reached 24 trillion pesos, while federal government income amounted to 12.6 trillion pesos—reducing their share of GDP from 17.4% in 1985 to 16.1% in 1986. However, excluding direct payments to the government by PEMEX, federal government revenues in 1986 increased to 9.6 trillion pesos as a consequence of fiscal measures adopted during that year.

In 1986, PEMEX contributions amounted to 23.4% of federal government income, income tax for 26.6%, VAT for 19.8%, excise taxes for 17.4%, trade taxes for 5.4% and other taxes for 1.5%. Miscellaneous revenues, amounting in 1986 to 6% of total federal receipts, were sharply up in that year due to increases in telephone charges and metro fares (previously set for years at around a ridiculously low one peso, irrespective of distance).

TABLE 3.7   MEXICAN PUBLIC SECTOR FINANCIAL POSITION 1982–1986

(% of GDP)	1982	1983	1984	1985	1986p
Total expenditures	46.5	42.7	41.5	40.7	45.4
Current	34.7	34.5	34.2	34.5	38.9
– wages and salaries	8.3	7.0	6.8	6.8	6.6
– interest payments	8.7	12.7	12.3	12.1	16.7
– other	17.7	14.8	15.1	15.6	15.6
Capital	10.8	7.7	6.9	5.6	5.6
Other	1.0	0.5	0.4	0.6	0.9
Total revenues	30.2	34.4	34.2	32.3	30.8
– PEMEX	10.9	14.8	13.4	12.0	9.2
– taxes	10.3	10.7	10.6	10.5	11.4
– other	9.0	8.9	10.2	9.8	10.2
ECONOMIC DEFICIT	16.3	8.3	7.3	8.4	15.2

Source: Banco de Mexico
Note: p – provisional

TABLE 3.8   FEDERAL GOVERNMENT RECEIPTS 1984–1986

(billion pesos)	1984	1985	1986p
PEMEX contributions	1707.7	2741.0	2936.1
Non-oil receipts	3267.1	5155.1	9615.1
– Taxes	3036.2	4750.2	8858.7
– income tax	1213.4	1890.1	3334.9
– VAT	942.8	1456.9	2479.5
– excise taxes	661.5	1019.5	2183.7
– trade taxes	143.1	279.8	671.7
– other	75.4	103.8	188.9
– Non-tax revenues	230.9	404.9	756.4
TOTAL	4974.8	7896.1	12551.2

Source: Banco de Mexico
Note: p – provisional

The 1987 budget, set in late 1986, envisages a cautious approach to the dire problems besetting the country after the falling oil price—and, indeed, represents nothing more than a caretaker budget until the presidential transfer of 1988. The fiscal plan envisages collection by the federal government of some 26.9 billion pesos in 1987, of which the oil sector is anticipated to contribute 10.7 billion pesos.

TABLE 3.9   FINANCIAL INCOME/EXPENDITURE ACCOUNTS FOR PEMEX
1984–1986

(billion pesos)	1984	1985	1986p
Income	3843.9	5463.7	7134.1
– Exports	2780.1	3845.3	3890.2
– Domestic revenue	910.2	1485.1	2911.1
– Other	153.6	133.3	332.7
Expenditure	3340.1	5045.0	7146.5
– Operational outlays	1061.4	1613.1	2958.1
– interest payments	474.8	463.9	831.9
– wages and salaries	151.3	277.9	512.4
– other	435.3	871.3	1613.8
– Taxes	1707.7	2741.0	2936.1
– Capital expenditure	469.1	598.0	953.2
– Other net flows	101.9	−92.9	−299.1
SURPLUS/DEFICIT	503.8	418.7	−12.4

Source: Banco de Mexico
Note: p – provisional

TABLE 3.10   FINANCIAL INCOME/EXPENDITURE ACCOUNTS FOR
OTHER GOVERNMENT AGENCIES 1984–1986

(billion pesos)	1984	1985	1986p
Income	3503.8	5466.3	8655.4
– Receipts	1814.3	2529.2	4455.2
– Transfers	1039.5	1767.4	2213.3
– Other	650.0	1169.7	1987.0
Expenditure	3793.1	5696.8	8894.5
– Operational outlays	3258.0	4847.5	7607.7
– interest payments	632.0	901.6	1357.3
– wages and salaries	707.3	1116.7	1804.5
– other	1918.7	2829.2	4445.9
– Taxes	19.9	28.2	38.1
– Capital expenditure	527.9	766.1	1136.0
– Other net flows	−12.7	55.0	112.0
DEFICIT	289.3	230.5	239.1

Source: Banco de Mexico
Note: p – provisional

Total public sector revenues—in the absence of any further massive external shock and, indeed, taking encouragement from the slightly better overall situation—are expected to rise by 2% as a proportion of GDP. Underpinning this growth are modest increases in taxation and rises in prices charged for public sector goods and utilities. Efforts are to be directed at enlarging the taxable base at the same time as actually reducing tax rates, and at strengthening tax collection and counter-evasion measures.

On the expenditure side, the 1987 budget envisages that total public expenditure will be reduced by the equivalent of 0.5% of GDP—although public investment should grow in real terms by 15% and by 0.5% of GDP. Accordingly, current expenditure is to be reduced by 1% of GDP from its already slimmed down 1986 level (in 1982 it stood at 18%). The government hopes to achieve this further reduction by lower transfers from the public sector and a reduction in non-financial expenditure other than wages. Furthermore, the availability of credit for the private sector (dramatically if not catastrophically squeezed during 1986) is planned to rise by 20% by an increase in public savings—which should reduce the use of domestic credit by the public sector.

For 1987 as a whole, total public expenditures of 86.2 trillion pesos are envisaged, of which non-programmatic expenditures will absorb 52.7 trillion pesos and programmatic expenditures some 33.5 trillion pesos. In the latter category of expenditure, 24% will be absorbed by health and educational programmes, 25.7% by the energy sector, 12.4% by the industrial sector, 10.2% by rural development and fisheries, 9.3% by transport and communications programmes, 5.7% by commerce and distribution, 5.4% by regional development and tourism programmes and 7.3% by the administrative and defence sectors.

One contingency mechanism built into the budget after skilful negotiation with the IMF and Mexico's main creditor banks is that if the export price of oil falls below US$9 a barrel, compensatory additional external financing for Mexico will be made available to the tune of US$1.8 billion—US$600 million from the IMF and US$1200 million from commercial banks. Agreed in recognition not only of the plight of Mexico but also the country's good intent, this deal has broken new ground and, combined with a growth contingency co-financing facility agreed with the World Bank and commercial financial institutions, has at least provided the outgoing administration of de la Madrid with extra room for manoeuvre in its wish for a five-month transition of power later in 1987.

TABLE 3.11   PROJECTED 1987 BUDGETARY REVENUE

(billion pesos)

Oil sector	10709.1
– PEMEX	7075.6
– Other	3633.5
Non-oil sector	16240.5
– Taxes	14458.5
– personal income tax	6862.5
– VAT	4300.5
– international trade	1537.7
– other	1757.7
– Non-tax revenue	1782.1
– rights	869.3
– other	912.8

Source: Secretaría de Hacienda y Crédito Público

VII   Money, banking, the Stock Market and the peso

The pivotal point of monetary policy and the Mexican financial system is the Banco de Mexico (central bank). The country's commercial banks were nationalized in a last-minute fit of further populism by the outgoing and now disgraced Lopez Portillo—although a return to the private sector should occur in coming years. The banking system has been consolidated, with the total number of institutions reduced to 19 in 1986 from 60 in 1982. The commercial banking system now comprises six nationwide 'clearing banks', five regional banks and eight multi-regional bodies. At the end of 1986 there were 4394 domestic bank branches, 19 foreign branches and 13 representative offices abroad.

National monetary policy is almost exclusively dictated by public sector financing requirements—during 1986, for instance, credit for the private sector was severely restricted under strictures imposed by the falling oil price, bank credit was channelled to the public sector and interest rates were sharply increased. The M1 measure of money supply accelerated during 1986 to reach 64.4% by December—although this represented (for the fourth year in a row) a reduction in real terms of the monetary base. In nominal terms the monetary base rose by 2.7 trillion pesos during 1986.

Consumer price inflation has been worryingly high for many years in Mexico. From a recent peak in 1983 when prices more than doubled, inflation fell to under 60% in 1985—only to re-accelerate in 1986. During 1987 inflation continued to rise, reaching 110% in February, 114% in March and 121% in April—all of which betrays the over-optimism implicit in the government's 80% target for 1987 as a whole.

TABLE 3.12   M1 AND INFLATION 1982–1986

(% change)	1982	1983	1984	1985	1986
M1[1]	62.1	41.3	63.0	51.2	64.4
Consumer price inflation[2]	59.0	101.8	65.5	57.8	84.5

Source: Banco de Mexico
Notes: [1] at year end
[2] annual average

The Mexican stock market has proved more active in recent years, with the total value of securities traded in 1986 rising by 68% in real terms. However, the stock market remains a relativey minor source of capital funds for Mexican business, with most concerns instead obtaining their finance from banks or by use of retained earnings. The stock exchange index rose from 14,203 at the end of January 1986 to 47,101 at the end of December in that year.

The national currency of Mexico, the peso, was sharply devalued in 1982 as the country realized the true implications of its intolerable borrowing level. From 24.5 pesos to the dollar in 1981, the rate shot to 120.1 pesos to the dollar by 1983. By 1986 the rate stood at 611.8 pesos to the dollar—and had halved again (around 1200 pesos) by the spring of 1987.

TABLE 3.13   THE PESO/DOLLAR EXCHANGE RATE 1981–1986

	1981	1982	1983	1984	1985	1986
Pesos/dollar	24.5	56.4	120.1	167.8	256.9	611.8

Source: IMF

VIII Post-colonial economic history

In 1821 the independence of Mexico was proclaimed by Iturbide. Then followed a century of turmoil and a build-up of foreign control of national assets. Following the traumatic loss of half of Mexico's national territory (a loss with which the country still has not psychologically or culturally come to terms) to the United States in 1868, the benevolent presidency of Benito Juárez involved in 1863–7 the occupation of the country by French troops. Benito Juárez, again gaining control with the ousting of the French, was succeeded after several years by the dictator Porfirio Diaz. Under the 35 years of Diaz's rule, the country experienced stability and economic prosperity at the price of massive corruption and the foreign (mainly British and later American) exploitation of the country's resources.

The Mexican revolution ensued—a decade-long period of turmoil, revolution and counter-revolution which laid the foundations for the most stable Latin-American society of modern times. In 1917 the current Mexican constitution was adopted and, in 1929, President Plutarco Calles founded the Partido Revolucionario Nacional (PRN), which has maintained a form of dictatorship over Mexico ever since, more recently as the PRI. The reforms of the aftermath of the revolutionary period, which had exhausted the country, were modest until the 1934–40 presidency of Lazaro Cardenas. Cardenas, a truly populist president, enacted land reform (ostensibly the cause of the revolution, but in fact more an ideal with which to manipulate the peasantry), nationalized the important oil industry and depoliticized the military—which has stayed out of politics for over half a century. Subsequent presidents have pursued equally populist policies, involving nationalization of the power supply, the railways, airlines and wides swathes of Mexican industry, as well as subsidizing staple foods and gasoline and establishing one of the developing world's best educational systems.

Since the Second World War, despite nationalist policies, and despite resentment felt in Mexico over the illegal occupation of Caribbean ports by US troops during the Cuban revolution of 1959, Mexican society has very broadly developed as a poor-relation mirror image of North America. Following the OPEC decision in 1974 to quadruple the price of oil, the country embarked on a massive borrowing and spending spree—a binge which has largely led to the economic crisis of the 1980s and which will hamper true paced development of Mexico until well into the next century. Popular at the time, the 12 years of rule under Echevarria and then Portillo—who now lives in self-imposed exile due to popular disgust at his gross corruption—are now regarded with dismay by all educated Mexicans who, until five years ago, were generally ultra-materialistic. In late 1982 the world debt crisis struck. Mexico had run up colossal debts, and the realization that much of the borrowed money had financed not only genuine development but also foreign bank accounts for government officials and 'white elephant' industrial projects of marginal use or even relevance to Mexico's structural problems only added to the mess in which the country found itself. The incumbent administration of Miguel de la Madrid inherited all these problems, in addition to an over-nationalized economy and a continuously growing and increasingly impoverished population.

IX   External debt and reserves

Mexico is almost impossibly in debt, owing broadly US$100 billion to foreign creditors. Much of the money was borrowed in the heady time before the boom in late 1982, although since that year—and during the crisis years—indebtedness has continued to rise sharply. The past two or three years have been characterized by rescheduling agreements, brinkmanship on the part of some Mexican finance officials, and the 1986 replacement as Finance Minister of Silva Herzog by Gustavo Petricioli. In July of that year, Mexico set a precedent—facilitated by its reputation for good intent and respon-sibility—by signing an agreement with the IMF allowing for contingency funding should the country's growth rate fail to match targets and should there be further reductions in the world oil price. In 1986 also, a major debt restructuring programme of debt amortization was put into action following protracted and very complicated negotiations with a host of Mexico's creditors. One further feature of the debt scene which developed in 1986 was the start of what could become a snowballing of debt for equity swaps, whereby creditors (realizing that their chances of recovering debt are realistically slim) exchange debt for shares in Mexican companies. Amounting to only a modest US$1.04 billion in 1986, during the first quarter of 1987 alone such swaps reached US$477 million and showed little sign of abating up to a (temporary?) suspension later in the year.

During 1987, incidentally, some major United States banks (and the Midland Bank of the United Kingdom) for the first time made realistic provision in their accounting position for bad debts made to developing countries in general (within which the Mexican problem, while unspecified, has played a substantial role). By the start of 1986, for instance, seven United States banks alone were owed US$13 billion by Mexico.

The near-intractable problem of Mexico's debt situation is illustrated by the fact that on an officially registered level of US$74 billion of bank and public external debt in 1986, interest payments amounted to US$6.13 billion, and amortization for a further US$4.78 billion. Accordingly, the debt service ratio (in relation to current revenues) in that year amounted to fully 45%—up sharply from the 36.5% of 1985 owing to the collapse in world oil prices. Really only the 1986 debt rescheduling programme, with extended amortization periods, offers Mexico (and its creditors?) a glimmer of hope—providing the oil price does not remain eternally as depressed as it was in 1986. Certainly, as 1987 progressed there was a marked easing of the country's foreign exchange situation.

TABLE 3.14   BANK AND PUBLIC SECTOR EXTERNAL DEBT 1979–1986

(US$ billion)	1979	1980	1981	1982	1983	1984	1985	1986p
Registered public debt								
Long-term	28.3	32.3	42.3	49.5	52.8	69.0	71.6	74.0
Short-term	1.5	1.5	10.8	9.3	9.8	0.4	0.5	1.4
TOTAL	29.8	33.8	53.0	58.8	62.6	69.4	72.1	75.4
Bank debt	2.6	5.1	7.0	8.0	10.3	6.2	4.8	5.5
TOTAL	32.4	38.9	60.0	66.8	72.9	75.6	76.9	80.9

Source: Secretaría de Hacienda y Crédito Público

TABLE 3.15   PUBLIC DEBT SERVICE 1979–1986

(US$ billion)	1979	1980	1981	1982	1983	1984	1985	1986p
Amortization	4.19	2.62	4.81	2.77	4.54	3.62	3.63	4.78
Interest payments	2.89	3.96	5.50	7.79	6.47	7.61	7.60	6.13
Debt service	7.07	6.58	10.30	10.56	11.01	11.23	11.23	10.91
Current revenues	16.26	24.95	30.81	28.00	28.95	32.90	30.77	24.27
Debt service ratio	43.50	26.40	33.40	37.70	38.00	34.10	36.50	45.00

Source: Secretaría de Hacienda y Crédito Público/Banco de Mexico

TABLE 3.16   PUBLIC EXTERNAL DEBT AMORTIZATION SCHEDULE

(US$ billion)	Before 1986 restructuring	After 1986 restructuring
1986	1208	258
1987	513	0
1988	1016	0
1989	3000	572
1990	3499	1897
1991	4291	1897
1992	4803	1897
1993	5293	1897
1994	5492	1606
1995	5582	1026
1996	5811	2623
1997	6091	1872
1998	6118	2666
1999	0	3182
2000	0	3672
2001	0	3652
2002	0	5609
2003	0	5839
2004	0	6120
2005	0	3072
2006	0	3072

Source: Secretaría de Hacienda y Crédito Público

TABLE 3.17   LEADING US BANKS' EXPOSURE TO MEXICO, START 1986

(US$ million)

Manufacturers Hanover	1802
BankAmerica	2709
Chase Manhattan	1680
Chemical New York	1471
Irving Bank	357
Citicorp	2800
Marine Midland	364
Bankers Trust New York	1277
Wells Fargo	606
First Chicago	912
JP Morgan	1250
Continental Illinois	555
Bank of Boston	245
Security Pacific	520
Republicbank	287
Mellon Bank	579
First Interstate	721

Source: IBCA

TABLE 3.18   AUTHORIZED MEXICAN DEBT-EQUITY SWAPS BY SECTOR
1986/1987

(US$ million)	1986	1987 1st quarter
Motor industry	449.6	20.3
Tourism	189.2	145.0
Capital goods	98.2	102.2
'Maquiladoras'	47.1	54.8
Chemical/pharmaceutical	59.9	16.8
Electronics	9.1	19.7
Agri-business	26.4	1.4
Textiles/shoes	0.8	20.0
Others	156.7	96.9
TOTAL	1037.0	477.1

Source: National foreign investments commission

Mexico's international reserves fell sharply during 1985 as imports
rose, although during 1986 they are provisionally estimated to have
increased as imports fell—to a point where they equated to around
seven months' import value.

TABLE 3.19   GROSS INTERNATIONAL RESERVES 1981–1986

(US$ million[1])		
	1981	5035
	1982	1832
	1983	4933
	1984	8134
	1985p	5806
	1986p	6791

Source: Banco de Mexico/Informe Anual
Note: [1] year end

X   Foreign policy

Mexico's foreign policy, and indeed its very perception of the outside
world, has for a century and more been conditioned by its powerful
northern neighbour. Relationships with the United States have never
been easy, although the geographical and economic facts of life have
forced both countries into an uneasy coexistence. Intervention in

Mexican affairs by the United States has coloured relations since the mid nineteenth century, with considerable over-sensitivity on the part of the modern Mexicans understandably prevalent. Feeling largely impotent in the face of US muscle, it is widely held by educated Mexicans (and privately by members of the Mexican Government) that such implied domination even prevents the establishment of true democracy in Mexico, in that any too left-of-centre government elected would be subverted by the United States, as has so often happened in less sensitive regions of Latin America. Nevertheless, the bourgeois behaviour of the middle classes of Mexico prior to the 1982 economic crisis, and their continuing aspirations, means that Mexican society itself in the last resort would do its utmost to avoid any left-wing take-over attempt.

On a day-to-day basis, Mexico and the United States have to seek to solve the common problem (or at least the US problem) of the flow of illegal immigrants and drugs across the extensive border, as well as to manage the country's debt situation and the massive exposure of US banks in the economy of their southern neighbour. Mexico is also keen to attract as much US investment as possible in the industrial sector, although in the longer term would like to increase European involvement in Mexican business life and to reduce its overdependence on the USA in foreign trading affairs.

Mexico is not a member of OPEC, despite being a leading world oil producer, but has preferred to reap the advantages of the higher world oil price after 1973 without any of the production quota responsibility which membership of OPEC would entail. The country has also—at least until 1986—steadfastly refused to join GATT, preferring instead to shelter behind high tariff walls and to export oil to the United States and to attract the latter's industrial overspill in order to gain foreign exchange. In recent years, however, there has been a growing realization that this is insufficient for the long-term development aims of Mexico, and last year the country at last joined GATT—although full integration will take several years. Mexico, which incidentally took a line independent of that of the United States over the Cuban revolution in 1959 by maintaining warm relations with Castro, is also a member of the Contadora group (including Venezuela, Colombia and Panama), which is seeking a compromise solution—again, unlike the strong policies of the United States—to the troubles of Central America. It is, however, of some interest that while Mexico welcomed the Sandinista revolution in Nicaragua, the country took a totally different line with its own southern neighbour, Guatemala (which is too close for comfort to the rural deprivation of southern Mexico), during the latter's problems in the early 1980s.

For the last 45 years and more, the Mexican armed forces have played a modest role in national life and have been totally subordinate to civilian wishes. The country actually spends less than one half of 1% of its GDP on defence, and its armed strength in fact is less than that of its small Central-American neighbours and certainly much less than that of Cuba. The role of the military is currently partly seen as one of suppression of drug trafficking, although if the problems of Central America reach overall eruption point, Mexico will probably expand its own modest military capability. Certainly, the political concensus in the country which has largely endured since the revolutionary era, combined with the existence of the world's greatest military power on its northern frontier, have ensured that the armed forces have kept a low profile both within and outside Mexico for decades.

XI   Foreign trade and balance of payments

Until the onset of the economic crisis in late 1982, Mexico had run a substantial deficit on its current account for many years as the country borrowed and spent with abandon. In 1981 the current account deficit reached a record US$16 billion, which owed its origins to massive public expenditure and to a grossly overvalued peso exchange rate which pushed up the level of interest and other payments to some US$8.4 billion, and thus more than negated the high level of exports. In 1982 the country was obliged to enact a crash devaluation of massive proportions, to block as many imports as possible and to instigate a truly severe austerity programme. These factors combined first to trim the current account deficit in 1982 and then to return the balance to positive over 1983–5. During 1986, however, a collapse in the dollar value of merchandise exports following the fall in the average price of oil, combined with the lack of external financing during the first seven months of the year, pushed the current account once more into deficit. The oil problem alone—according to the Banco de Mexico—sliced some US$8.5 billion from Mexico's foreign exchange earnings during 1986, a sum equivalent to a staggering 6.7% of GDP. Nevertheless, the position would have been worse had it not been for a 41% increase in non-oil exports and a modest decline in international interest rates (which reduced interest payments on Mexico's debt).

TABLE 3.20   MEXICAN BALANCE OF PAYMENTS 1981–1986

(US$ billion)	1981	1982	1983	1984	1985p	1986p
Merchandise exports	20.10	21.23	22.31	24.20	21.66	16.03
Merchandise imports	23.95	14.44	8.55	11.25	13.21	11.43
Current account balance	−16.05	−6.22	5.42	4.24	1.24	−1.27
Capital account balance	23.21	6.75	−1.11	0.04	−1.53	2.27

Source: Banco de Mexico
Note: p – provisional

Around two-thirds of Mexico's foreign exchange in 1986 derived from merchandise exports—down from the three-quarters of 1982–3. Tourism, border transactions, Mexico's in-bond industries (the 'maquiladoras') and miscellaneous factors, such as inward investment, financial services and capital repatriation by companies and individuals, have all come to account for higher proportions of foreign exchange income.

TABLE 3.21   STRUCTURE OF MEXICO'S FOREIGN EXCHANGE EARNINGS 1981–1986

(%)	1981	1982	1983	1984	1985p	1986p
Exports	63.0	75.8	77.1	73.5	70.4	66.1
Tourism	5.7	5.0	5.6	5.9	5.6	7.4
Border transactions	15.5	4.4	3.8	4.0	3.8	4.9
In-bond industries	3.2	2.9	2.8	3.5	4.1	5.3
Others	12.6	11.9	10.7	13.1	16.1	16.3

Source: Banco de Mexico
Note: p – provisional

Mexican exports have—until 1986 at least—broadly maintained their dollar value in recent years, despite the massive 1982 devaluation of the peso. This has been due to pricing of oil sales in dollars and to a rise in the level of non-oil merchandise exports by Mexico. In 1986, however, as intimated, exports collapsed, as did the oil price—although imports remained modest (in pre-recessionary terms). The annual average price of oil exported by Mexico fell from US$25.35 a barrel in 1985 to only US$11.87 a barrel in 1986—which alone explains Mexico's plunge back into recession in that year. For the first time in very many years, the value of manufactured goods exports exceeded that of petroleum products sales abroad, with crude oil exports in 1986 totalling only US$5.58 billion. Agricultural products have also come to take a greatly enhanced relative share of

TABLE 3.22   STRUCTURE OF MERCHANDISE EXPORTS 1981–1986

(%)	1981	1982	1983	1984	1985p	1986p
Minerals and oil	74.7	78.2	74.1	65.0	63.8	38.0
Manufactured products	17.7	16.0	20.6	28.9	29.7	48.9
Agricultural products	7.6	5.8	5.3	6.1	6.5	13.1

Source: Banco de Mexico
Note: p – preliminary

TABLE 3.23   MAIN PRODUCTS EXPORTED 1984–1986

(% of total)	1984	1985	1986p
Crude oil	61.8	61.4	34.8
Automobiles and transport equipment	6.5	7.3	14.5
Chemical products	3.1	3.1	3.9
Coffee	1.7	2.3	5.1
Frozen shrimps	1.7	1.5	neg
Silver (in bars)	1.4	1.2	1.9
Iron and steel	1.6	1.1	2.8
Fuel oil	0.9	1.0	1.0
Textile and leather goods	1.1	0.9	2.1
Tomatoes	0.9	1.0	2.5
Cattle	0.5	0.9	1.6
Petrochemical products	0.7	0.5	0.5
Cotton	0.9	0.4	0.5
Natural gas	0.9	–	–
Others	16.3	17.4	28.8
TOTAL	100.0	100.0	100.0

Source: Banco de Mexico
Notes: p – preliminary
        neg – negligible

exports, and, indeed, in dollar terms rose by 51% in 1986. Of manufactured products, exports of vehicles and components (especially engines) in 1986 exceeded US$1 billion, while sales of coffee amounted to US$825 million.

TABLE 3.24   VALUE OF LEADING EXPORTS[1] 1986

	US$ million	Growth rate 1985–1986
Agricultural products, livestock and fisheries		
Coffee	824.5	67.7
Tomatoes	407.7	90.4
Cattle	264.8	41.6
Minerals and oil		
Crude oil	5580.2	−58.1
Copper	162.0	9.2
Sulphur	134.8	19.3
Manufactures		
Automobile motors	1152.7	10.9
Automobiles	516.4	343.6
Frozen shrimps	353.8	9.6
Silver (in bars)	308.1	17.7
Manufactured iron or steel	211.8	126.8
Gas oil	211.5	2.1
Textile fibres	153.3	78.7

Source: Banco de Mexico
Note: [1] all figures are preliminary

Merchandise imports to Mexico collapsed in 1982–3, reducing in dollar terms by two-thirds between 1981 and 1983 due in part to the peso devaluation and to a much more restrictive official import policy. Since 1985 the country has started to liberalize its economy with its entry to GATT, although imports actually fell sharply in 1986. Even so, intermediate goods (i.e. parts such as automobile components for assembly and possible subsequent re-export) dominate the pattern of importing, accounting in 1985 for around two-thirds of all imports. Consumer goods imports are still effectively negligible, which reflects the highly protectionist tradition which has dominated Mexican imports for years. Machinery and transport equipment imports comprise the largest single component of Mexican imports of goods.

TABLE 3.25 STRUCTURE OF MERCHANDISE IMPORTS 1981–1985

(%)	1981	1982	1983	1984	1985p
Intermediate inputs	56.6	58.3	67.1	69.6	67.9
Capital goods	31.7	31.2	25.7	22.9	23.9
Consumer goods	11.7	10.5	7.2	7.5	8.2

Source: Banco de Mexico
Note: p – preliminary

TABLE 3.26 MAIN PRODUCTS IMPORTED 1985 AND 1986

(% of total)	1985	1986p
Parts for electrical installations	2.3	3.1
Automobile parts	2.2	2.1
Butane and propane gas	2.4	1.5
Soyabean seeds	2.1	1.5
Sorghum	2.0	0.7
Corn	1.9	1.4
Pumps, motor pumps and turbo pumps	1.9	1.4
Ships, parts and marine equipment	1.8	2.9
Metalwork machinery	1.6	2.0
Cellulose paste for paper	1.4	1.7
Generators, transformers and electrical motors	1.1	1.3
Agricultural fertilizers	0.9	0.7
Powdered milk	0.8	1.0
Sugar	neg	neg
Others	77.6	78.7
TOTAL	100.0	100.0

Source: Banco de Mexico
Notes: p – preliminary
neg – negligible

The direction of Mexico's foreign trade is inextricably linked with the country's giant northern neighbour, and a desire to diversify both markets for Mexican products and sources of supply of imports (and capital). In 1986 the United States accounted for almost two-thirds of the total value of Mexican trade—both inbound and outbound—which, if anything, represented a modest relative advance over the levels of 1982/3. Western Europe—and especially Spain (Mexico's third trading partner)—and Japan are also important to the Mexican external economy. In 1986 the United States is provisionally estimated by the Banco de Mexico to have supplied imports valued at

TABLE 3.27 VALUE OF LEADING IMPORTS[1] 1986

	US$ million	Growth rate 1985–1986
Agricultural products, livestock and fisheries		
Corn	165.5	−0.35
Soyabean seeds	167.2	−0.39
Minerals and oil		
Phosphorite and calcium phosphate	29.9	9.5
Manufactures		
Parts for electrical installations	355.3	16.8
Ships, parts and marine equipment	336.5	36.9
Metalwork machinery	224.6	−17.1
Mixtures and preparations for industrial use	212.5	−6.3
Cellulose paste for paper	198.5	9.1

Source: Banco de Mexico
Note: [1] all figures are preliminary

US$7.4 billion to Mexico and to have purchased Mexican goods to the value of US$10.6 billion—both directly as direct exports and indirectly under the 'maquiladora' scheme.

TABLE 3.28 MEXICO'S MAJOR TRADING PARTNERS 1982–1986

(%)	1982	1983	1984	1985	1986p
Exports					
Western hemisphere	61.0	69.3	67.8	69.1	74.9
– United States	50.6	58.6	57.8	61.9	66.1
– Canada	2.5	2.2	2.3	1.9	1.2
– Latin-American Integration Association[1]	4.5	4.4	4.0	3.0	4.0
Argentina	0.3	0.3	0.3	0.2	0.8
Brazil	3.0	3.0	2.5	1.5	1.1
Venezuela	0.3	0.2	0.2	0.2	0.3
Others	0.9	0.9	1.0	1.1	1.8
– Central American Common Market[2]	2.5	2.6	2.3	1.3	1.3
– Others	0.9	1.6	1.4	2.0	2.3
Western Europe	20.2	19.0	19.7	19.1	14.3
– European Economic Community[3]	9.8	10.2	11.2	10.1	13.1
– European Free Trade Association[4]	0.9	1.2	1.1	0.7	1.1
– Spain	7.9	7.4	7.2	7.9	0.0
– Others	1.6	0.2	0.2	0.4	0.1

TABLE 3.28   MEXICO'S MAJOR TRADING PARTNERS 1982–1986 *continued*

(%)	1982	1983	1984	1985	1986p
Asia	11.1	11.0	11.8	11.5	9.7
– Japan	6.4	6.9	8.0	8.0	6.6
– Others	4.7	4.1	3.8	3.5	3.1
Rest of the world	5.8	0.6	0.7	0.3	1.2
– Eastern Europe	0.2	0.2	0.3	0.2	0.3
– Others	5.6	0.4	0.4	0.1	0.9
TOTAL	100.0	100.0	100.0	100.0	100.0
Imports					
Western hemisphere	69.9	72.2	72.7	72.8	71.4
– United States	62.1	65.0	65.4	65.6	65.0
– Canada	2.2	2.9	2.2	1.8	1.9
– Latin-American Integration Association[1]	3.8	2.5	4.1	4.4	3.1
Argentina	0.9	0.4	1.5	2.1	1.4
Brazil	2.4	1.6	2.1	1.6	1.3
Venezuela	0.1	0.1	0.1	0.1	0.1
Others	0.4	0.4	0.4	0.6	0.3
– Central American Common Market[2]	0.9	1.0	0.4	0.3	0.2
– Others	0.8	0.8	0.5	0.7	1.2
Western Europe	21.0	18.7	17.5	16.2	19.3
– European Economic Community[3]	14.7	13.9	12.4	11.4	15.4
– European Free Trade Association[4]	3.0	2.2	2.6	2.6	3.3
– Spain	2.6	2.0	1.8	1.6	0.0
– Others	0.7	0.6	0.7	0.6	0.6
Asia	7.8	5.7	5.9	6.9	7.6
– Japan	5.9	4.4	4.6	5.6	6.0
– Others	1.9	1.3	1.3	1.3	1.6
Rest of the world	1.3	3.4	3.9	4.1	1.7
– Eastern Europe	0.3	0.2	0.2	0.4	0.6
– Others	1.0	3.2	3.7	3.7	1.1
TOTAL	100.0	100.0	100.0	100.0	100.0

Source: Banco de Mexico
Notes: [1] The Latin-American Integration Association comprises Argentina, Brazil, Bolivia, Colombia, Chile, Ecuador, Paraguay, Peru, Uruguay and Venezuela
[2] The Central American Common Market comprises Costa Rica, El Salvador, Guatemala, Honduras and Nicaragua
[3] The European Economic Community comprises West Germany, Belgium/Luxembourg, Denmark, France, Ireland, Italy, Greece, United Kingdom, the Netherlands, Spain and Portugal
[4] The European Free Trade Association comprises Austria, Finland, Norway, Portugal, Sweden, Switzerland and Iceland
p – preliminary

TABLE 3.29   MEXICO–UNITED STATES TRADE BALANCE 1982–1986

(US$ million)	1982	1983	1984	1985	1986p
Exports	10743.1	12981.1	13704.1	13145.5	10603.1
Imports	8969.3	5519.6	7315.0	8633.1	7391.9
Trade balance	1773.8	7461.5	6389.1	4512.4	3211.2

Source: Banco de Mexico
Note: p – preliminary

TABLE 3.30   MEXICO–EEC TRADE BALANCE 1982–1986

(US$ million)	1982	1983	1984	1985	1986p
Exports	2590.0	2286.9	2659.0	2173.8	2106.8
Imports	2222.2	1184.0	1385.7	1503.1	1757.1
Trade balance	367.8	1102.9	1273.3	670.7	349.7

Source: Banco de Mexico
Note: p – preliminary

TABLE 3.31   MEXICO-JAPAN TRADE BALANCE 1982–1986

(US$ million)	1982	1983	1984	1985	1986p
Exports	1450.3	1535.2	1905.0	1719.5	1057.2
Imports	854.5	372.7	518.5	734.8	683.1
Trade balance	595.8	1162.5	1386.5	984.7	374.1

Source: Banco de Mexico
Note: p – preliminary

XII   Agriculture

Mexico is a major agricultural producer and (in some produce areas) exporter, with the agricultural sector one of the mainstays of the entire Mexican economy. The country has, however, yet to become fully self-sufficient in particular sectors (notably some grains and beef), while agricultural policies are a potential flash-point for national unrest. The efficiency of agricultural operations in Mexico is generally low by European or North-American standards, with the major exceptions being the super-productive and irrigated vegetable gardens close to the United States frontier which operate primarily under an export-oriented policy.

The organization of the Mexican agricultural system is of some importance, as conditions on the land provide one of the keys to an understanding of Mexico's collective national psyche. Ostensibly a peasants' revolt against the *hacienda* system of Mexico, the revolutionary era culminated in Cardenas' land reform during the 1930s. This ushered in the *ejidos*, or village commune pattern of landholding, which has since characterized the farming system over much of the country. Approximately half of Mexico's agricultural land is now farmed on an *ejido* basis, which gives land to peasants in perpetuity on condition that they farm it for themselves. Despite their original social advantages over the *hacienda* or large estate system which they replaced, the *ejidos* are now highly inefficient and allow nothing more than subsistence cropping on small plots, or *minifundios*, for millions of rural labourers. Furthermore, the bulk of the non-*ejido* farms are also tiny and provide nothing more than a bare minimum living for their owners. Only a few estates and some export-oriented farms (such as the irrigated market gardens of northern Mexico) can actually meet international standards of agricultural competitivity. Nevertheless, the present system seems likely to endure, given its roots in the revolution and the opportunities for political control and co-operation of the peasantry which it has offered successive Mexican presidents.

Alleviation of rural poverty is at least seen as an important policy by the de la Madrid administration, which has launched the Pronaderi programme for rural development in an attempt to help stem continued migration to Mexico's swollen cities. In many ways, somehow upgrading living standards in the countryside will be the only effective means of continuing the long-term stability of the Mexican political system.

In 1985 agriculture accounted for 8.8% of Mexico's GDP, compared to 8.5% in 1984. Over 1983–6 the importance of this sector has increased modestly as the star of oil and gas has fallen, although in the longer term agricultural produce has become rather less important than hitherto (back in 1970, for instance, it contributed 12.2% to GDP). It is, however, not merely as a component of the national economic system of Mexico that the agricultural sector is important. It is also a major employer, second only to the service sector, and accounted for 29% of the total Mexican labour force in 1984. During 1986 agricultural production fell by 4.2%, owing to a reduction in the cultivated area, to poor weather conditions and to a lower level of water available for irrigation. Exports of agricultural goods in 1986 amounted to a provisionally estimated 13–14% of total Mexican exports, up from 10% in 1984 and providing a measure of comfort for a country hard pressed to earn foreign exchange in the wake of the collapsed oil price. Nevertheless, despite the high level of agricutural employment—or, in fact, because of it—value-added in this sector is very low (less than one-third that of Mexican manufacturing industry), and rural poverty extreme.

Mexico's agricultural sectors are divisible into those where the country is a net importer and those where output is partly (or primarily) export oriented. The country is both a major producer of grain crops and a rearer of domesticated animals, although in both these areas imports are substantial. Provisional estimates suggest that output of grains in 1986 was up to 20% lower than in 1985, although grain imports were much lower than in pre-crisis 1982. Maize is by far the most important crop grown in Mexico, and is in fact the staple food for millions of poor Mexicans. Production fell by 18–19% in 1986, with output of wheat in contrast declining much less sharply. Sorghum, beans, rice and soya beans are all important food crops in Mexico.

Mexico's head of cattle numbered around 38 million 1985, with beef production nevertheless insufficient to keep pace with demand, owing in part to the high cost of feed on the extensive arid and semi-arid lands of the North. The country is, therefore, a net beef importer—a far cry from the days when Mexico was a net beef exporter (to the United States in particular). The national total head of pigs and chickens (especially) is also very substantial indeed.

Mexico is a notable exporter of coffee, which in fact accounts for the greatest individual crop share of agricultural export revenue. After a record 4.8 million bags collected in 1983/4, output fell sharply in 1984/5 to recover in 1985/6 to a broadly similar level. Exports of coffee rose sharply in 1986 (growing by 80% in the first six months of the year alone), with higher world prices in part responsible.

Cotton and sugar are also important sectors of Mexico's agricultural economy. With around 200,000 hectares under cotton cultivation, production in 1985/6 was of the broad order of one million bales (albeit down on the 1.25 million bales of 1984/5 and at the same approximate level as the 1.04 million bales of 1983/4). Cotton exports in 1984/5 amounted to 430,000 bales, with a provisional fall believed to have taken place during 1985/6. A shift towards grain crop cultivation has reduced the land area planted with cotton during the past two or three years. Sugar production in 1984/5 was 3.25 million

TABLE 3.32   MAIN AGRICULTURAL PRODUCTS 1982–1986

('000)	1982		1983		1984		1985		1986p	
	h	t	h	t	h	t	h	t	h	t
Corn	8377	10129	8638	13061	7978	12932	8278	13869	8152	11316
Beans	2448	943	2262	1282	2039	974	2065	912	2322	986
Rice	207	511	165	416	153	484	281	804	194	539
Wheat	1011	4038	907	3460	1079	4505	2281	5207	1284	4769
Sorghum	1678	4717	1977	4846	1885	4974	2045	6564	1920	4802
Barley	311	396	327	557	311	619	299	541	315	513
Soyabeans	412	648	416	686	426	685	500	940	405	706
Sesame	133	32	183	87	157	61	160	71	124	51
Carthamus	228	221	458	277	256	209	298	150	258	161

Source: Secretaría de Agricultura y Recursos Hidraulicos/Banco de Mexico
Notes: p – preliminary
       h – hectares
       t – tonnes

TABLE 3.33   MAIN AGRICULTURAL EXPORTS 1982–1986

(US$ million)	1982	1983	1984	1985	1986p
Cotton	183.8	115.7	208.2	90.2	74.1
Coffee	345.1	385.7	424.4	491.6	824.5
Fresh fruits	72.1	47.6	81.6	89.6	116.0
Vegetables	178.4	149.5	179.3	161.6	197.9
Tobacco	46.8	20.5	27.2	25.8	28.4
Tomatoes	153.9	112.3	220.7	214.1	407.7

Source: Banco de Mexico
Note: p – preliminary

tonnes, with output being increased considerably in recent years due to government reorganization and expansion of the industry with a rationalization of old uneconomic mills and the construction of new efficient plant. In 1985/6 sugar output is provisionally estimated to have expanded further to around 3.7 million tonnes.

The importance of vegetable growing on irrigated farms in northern Mexico has already been commented on; the country is also a major citrus fruit and banana producer.

Forestry is also a major user of land in Mexico. Approximately 50 million hectares of the country are forested, with the north west particularly densely covered. Wood pulp, construction timber and fuel are the major uses of timber, with the country however remaining a net importer owing to over-exploitation of some domestic reserves. A major programme of reafforestation has been under way for several years.

If sectors of the Mexican forest have been over-exploited, the same cannot be said of the country's coastal fisheries potential. The potential on the Gulf of Mexico coast has scarcely been scratched, while only a few per cent of Pacific coast potential is as yet tapped (and then partly by North-American and Japanese boats). Nevertheless, the government has initiated a programme of investment in national fisheries, coupled with an exhortation to Mexicans to eat more fish. The plan, however, which supposes a doubling of the national fish catch by the late 1980s, is probably over-optimistic (in 1986, for instance, the catch increased by only a few per cent). Tuna, sardines, oysters and shrimps are among the fish and seafood earning at least some export revenue for Mexico.

XIII   Energy

The economic history of Mexico of the past two decades and more has been inextricably linked with national and international energy issues. Until the early 1970s the country's energy policy reflected the relatively cheap crude oil price which characterized the pre-OPEC days, with domestic subsidies high and successive governments concerned to keep prices to consumers (individual and corporate) to a minimum. In consequence, the state oil and gas monopoly Petroleos Mexicanos (PEMEX) not only ran up high debts and was unable to embark upon a full exploration programme, but by 1973 Mexico had even become a net importer of petroleum and petroleum products.

In 1972/3, however, the country's fortunes in this respect were dramatically improved by two events—although in a mishandled fashion which led directly to the current dire plight in which Mexico finds itself. First, in 1972 the very richly endowed Reforma oil field was discovered. Second, in late 1973 OPEC abruptly quadrupled the crude oil price. This led, however, to a burgeoning in the national level of foreign debt as the country embarked upon a spending and borrowing spree—always secured against an assumed further sustained increase in the world oil price. Coupled with a continuation of heavy price subsidies for Mexicans, the scene was set for the effective economic calamity of late 1982.

61

Since the onset of crisis, Mexico has adopted several points of note in its overall energy policy. First has been to continue to remain outside of OPEC, but to continue to follow closely the latter's pricing policy. Second, to maintain a broad ceiling on petroleum exports of 1.5 million barrels/day in a co-operation policy with OPEC (in 1986, for instance, they averaged 1.3 million barrels/day). Third, to avoid speculation on the Rotterdam spot market in an attempt to create some semblance of price stability in Mexico's own market. Fourth, to increase exports of petroleum products. Fifth, to diversify its export base in geographical terms, to reduce dependence on the United States (which regularly purchases around half of all Mexican petroleum exports). Sixth, to explore for new oil fields in order to maintain a minimum 70 billion barrel reserve base. Seventh—and, most important of all from the point of view of national self-discipline—a phasing out of, or at least a sharp reduction in, domestic price subsidies.

As intimated, Mexico's oil reserves in 1986 amounted to around 70 billion barrels—equivalent to around 75 years' worth of current production. Since the late 1970s the country's reserves have risen sharply, although they have been trimmed since the peak level of 1983. Despite PEMEX's earlier policy of artificially inflating proven reserve levels (some observers have attributed this to a desire to extract ready loans from the international financial community prior to 1982), the country is clearly blessed with ample—indeed abundant—known reserves, with sizeable fields likely to be discovered in the future. Gas reserves amount to more than 15 billion cubic feet (more than 50 years' production equivalent).

TABLE 3.34   MEXICO'S OIL RESERVES 1979–1986

	1979	1980	1981	1982	1983	1984	1985	1986p
Volume (bn barrels)	45.8	60.0	72.0	72.0	72.5	71.8	69.2	70.0

Source: PEMEX
Note: p – preliminary

Actual oil production levels have fallen from a peak of more than one billion barrels in 1982, although they have remained relatively strong in the face of healthy United States demand. Gas output has performed rather less well since (again) the peak production levels of 1982. Overall, export levels in 1985–6 were down on those of 1982–4, with the total foreign exchange earned by Mexico from the oil and gas sectors collapsing from US$14.53 billion in 1985 to US$6.1 billion in 1986—due in part to the collapse in the world oil price (which fell by 50% in the first quarter of the year alone). This has itself triggered a fresh economic crisis for Mexico, with the oil sector on its own no longer able to cover even interest charges on the country's international debt. In 1986 the United States accounted for 50.6% of Mexican oil exports, Spain for 15.2%, Japan for 14.1%, France for 6.3% and Israel for 3%.

TABLE 3.35   CRUDE OIL AND GAS PRODUCTION 1979–1986

	1979	1980	1981	1982	1983	1984	1985	1986p
Crude oil (mn barrels)	542	709	844	1002	973	983	960	886
Gas (mn ft³/ day)	2951	3548	4061	4246	4054	3753	3604	3431

Source: PEMEX
Note: p – preliminary

TABLE 3.36   CRUDE OIL AND NATURAL GAS EXPORTS 1979–1986

	1979	1980	1981	1982	1983	1984	1985	1986p
Crude oil (mn barrels)	194	302	401	545	561	566	524	471
Gas (mn ft³/day)	n.a.	281	288	273	217	148	n.a.	n.a.

Source: PEMEX
Notes: p – preliminary
       n.a. – not available

TABLE 3.37   VALUE OF MEXICO'S OIL AND GAS EXPORTS 1979–1986

	1979	1980	1981	1982	1983	1984	1985	1986p
US$ billion	3.99	10.43	14.57	16.45	16.02	16.33	14.53	6.10

Source: PEMEX
Note: p – preliminary

Mexico's other sources of raw energy are modest. Coal output runs at seven to eight million tonnes per annum, while sugar cane bagasse is used in some coastal regions as boiler fuel. Firewood production is not inconsiderable; neither is it, however, particularly important to the country's energy balance.

Mexico's electricity generating capacity has increased on an annual basis for some considerable time, growing by almost one-fifth since 1982 alone to stand at virtually 22 million kilowatts in 1986. The bulk of the increase has come from thermal power station construction, with a second coal-fired station planned and with gas-powered plant now favoured above oil-fuelled. Actual demand for electricity reached almost 90 billion kilowatt hours in 1986. Mexico also produces a modest amount of geothermal electricity, and in 1986 revived the mothballed (in 1982), vastly over-budget Laguna Verde nuclear power plant. There are, however, no plans to restore the over-ambitious Portillo programme for nuclear generation.

TABLE 3.38   ELECTRICITY CAPACITY AND GENERATION 1981–1986

	1981	1982	1983	1984	1985	1986p
Generating capacity (million kilowatts)						
Hydro-electric	6.5	6.6	6.5	6.5	6.5	6.7
Thermal-electric	10.9	11.8	12.5	12.9	14.3	14.9
TOTAL	17.4	18.4	19.0	19.4	20.8	21.6
Generation (billion kilowatts/hour)						
Hydro-electric	24.4	22.7	20.6	23.4	26.1	19.9
Thermal-electric	43.5	50.5	54.2	56.1	59.2	69.5
TOTAL	67.9	73.2	74.8	79.5	85.3	89.4

Source: Comision Federal de Electricidad
Note: p – preliminary

XIV   Mining

Mexico possesses substantial mineral resources and is amongst the world's five leading producers of more than a dozen minerals. The sector, which accounts for 3–3.5% of GDP, rivals tourism and the 'maquiladora' industries of the border zone for second place behind oil and gas as an export earner for Mexico. Extraction of silver has continued since the days of Cortes (and indeed before), and Mexico is the world's leading producer of this precious metal. The country is well blessed with reserves of non-ferrous metals, is an important copper, zinc and lead producer (the two latter often mined in conjunction with silver), and also a notable source of molybdenum (mined in association with copper). Mexico is, however, a modest (around five million tonnes per annum) producer of iron ore. Manganese is also mined in Mexico, as is gold.

With the 1982 nationalization of the country's banks, control of much of the mining industry passed into state hands. In 1984, however, the sale by Bancomer of its 70% stake in La Minera Frisco, as well as of shares in lesser mining groups, reduced the government's holdings in the Mexican mining industry to around 40%. Foreign participation in this sector is modest, with private sector Mexican interest predominating.

Although the de la Madrid administration has placed considerable stress upon the development of the country's mineral resources, low world prices for some key minerals (and notably for copper) have hampered expansion plans at the Mexicana de Cobre's Caridad and Cananea mines in Sonora. Silver exploration is, in contrast, proceeding apace, with such groups as Industrial Minera Mexico

TABLE 3.39   VOLUME OF MINING PRODUCTION—MAIN PRODUCTS
1982–1986

	1982	1983	1984	1985	1986p
Precious metals					
Gold (kg)	6104	6930	6998	7524	7804
Silver (tonnes)	1550	1911	1987	2153	2308
Industrial non-ferrous metals ('000 tonnes)					
Lead	146	167	183	207	183
Copper	239	206	189	168	175
Zinc	232	257	290	275	271
Siderurgical metals and minerals ('000 tonnes)					
Coke	2796	2812	2721	2725	2594
Iron	5382	5306	5489	5161	4903
Manganese	183	133	181	151	170
Non-metallic minerals ('000 tonnes)					
Sulphur	1815	1602	1820	2020	2050
Fluor spar	631	557	627	697	737
Baryta	324	357	426	468	312

Source: Secretaría de Programación y Presupuesto
Note: p – preliminary

taking a leading role. Total production in the mining sector contracted by 4.1% in 1986 due to a sharp fall in domestic demand—while exports stagnated.

XV Manufacturing industry

During the three decades 1950–1980, successive Mexican governments fostered rapid industrialization of their country as a means not only to fuel growth and national pride, but also in order to mop up as much of the burgeoning potential workforce as possible—albeit at very low rates of remuneration by the standards of industrialized countries. During those three decades, rates of growth in manufacturing output averaged an impressive 7–8% per annum. Industry was based where possible on import substitution policies, with multinational concerns from abroad encouraged to establish or develop manufacturing facilities, most especially in sectors where some form of technology transfer could be considered (e.g. automobiles, tyres, pharmaceuticals and, more recently, data processing). Where Mexico was able to take advantage of its abundant natural resources–as in the oil, petrochemical, paper, textile, non-ferrous metals and steel industries–conglomerates were the preferred means of exploitation.

Over 1970–86 as a whole, industrial output effectively doubled—although after the peak of 1981, production slumped, as did the economy. In 1985 a resurgence was in evidence to an all-time record level, although the recovery proved short-lived. During 1986 output contracted by 4–5%, as did total GDP, in the wake of the oil price crisis. Up to 1986 the petrochemical and heavy motor components (especially engines) industries were especially buoyant sectors of the manufacturing economy.

During 1986 none of the leading industrial branches recorded a positive growth, with the greatest reduction of all (at 13%) occurring in the major metal products and machinery industry. Despite growth in the volume of exports in the manufacturing sector of some 27% in 1986, this did not compensate fully for a 6.9% reduction in domestic Mexican demand. Accordingly, in 1986 Mexican manufacturing industry was able to operate at only 77% of installed capacity. In the consumer goods sector output fell by 3% by volume due to a decline in private consumption—output of consumer durables fell by 11.1%

and that of the more essential non-durables by 1.4%. Production of capital goods contracted by fully 12.8% in 1986.

TABLE 3.40   MANUFACTURING INDUSTRIAL PRODUCTION 1979–1986

	1979	1980	1981	1982	1983	1984	1985	1986p
Index (1970=100)	185.9	199.3	213.3	207.1	192.0	202.7	215.0	205.2
Growth rate (%)	10.6	7.2	7.0	−2.9	−7.3	5.6	6.1	−4.6

Source: Banco de Mexico
Note: p – provisional

TABLE 3.41   EVOLUTION OF MAJOR SECTORS OF INDUSTRIAL OUTPUT 1970–1985

	1970	1984	1985
Sugar refining	100.0	143.9	149.9
Oil refining	100.0	258.5	260.4
Petrochemicals	100.0	544.3	555.8
Cement	100.0	256.8	288.0
Iron smelting	100.0	232.3	214.9
Steel smelting	100.0	194.0	188.1
Automobiles and trucks	100.0	195.6	248.0
Engines for above	100.0	445.2	502.4

Source: Banco de Mexico

TABLE 3.42   PRODUCTION OF INDUSTRIAL SUBSECTORS 1970–1986

(index: 1970=100)	1970	1981	1982	1983	1984	1985	1986
Food, drink and tobacco	100.0	177.0	175.0	184.0	186.7	195.1	189.5
Textiles and clothing	100.0	186.1	178.2	157.2	174.1	167.1	162.6
Wood products	100.0	196.6	194.6	164.2	169.5	175.8	161.6
Paper, printing and publishing	100.0	209.5	204.6	193.3	199.1	220.8	209.0
Chemicals and plastics	100.0	279.1	255.3	264.1	294.2	302.4	294.7
Non-metallic minerals	100.0	202.1	163.0	170.0	196.8	197.8	171.8
Base metals	100.0	207.1	171.1	186.2	205.1	205.6	172.0
Metalworking and engineering	100.0	249.4	178.5	154.8	185.1	200.9	162.9
Other manufacturing	100.0	188.6	163.5	155.0	169.3	178.1	165.2
ALL MANUFACTURING	100.0	215.0	191.3	187.5	204.8	212.0	196.9

Source: Banco de Mexico

Before briefly observing individual major sectors of Mexican industry, it is of interest to comment on the 'in-bond' or 'maquiladora' phenomenon of the border zone. Set up in the 1960s, the in-bond industry has taken off since the 1982 economic crisis, and massive peso devaluation made it extremely attractive for American corporations to set up assembly plants along the Mexican side of the frontier zone at cities such as Juarez. Such 'maquiladoras' produce goods primarily for export to the United States and further afield, and are encouraged by the Mexican Government owing to their job-creation and foreign exchange-earning potential. The attractiveness for US corporations lies in the very low rates of pay (at under US$1 per hour) they need to offer, with in-bond development proceeding apace, despite claims by protectionist and unionist groups in the United States that such schemes have cost more than 300,000 American jobs.

In 1986 the 'maquiladora' sector earned Mexico foreign exchange of some US$1.4 billion—up by 6% on the level of 1985—and is expected to bring the country more than US$1.5 billion during 1987. 1986 also saw a 25% rise in the total number of in-bond plants to over 1000, with employment increasing by nearly one-fifth to some 250,000. More recently, two further developments have character-ized the 'maquiladora' sector of Mexico's manufacturing economy. First has been the interest of Japanese and European firms (British companies alone are considering investing over £100 million in Mexico in 1987 alone), as well as US companies, in developing in-bond interests. Second has been a geographical shift away from the border for some new plants, which have instead located in the poor and remote southern provinces of Yucatan and Oaxaca. In 1986 more than 100 non-border 'maquiladora' firms employed almost 40,000 workers, attracted by a dispensation allowing them to sell up to 40% of their manufactures within Mexico instead of being obliged to export almost all of their output.

It now remains to discuss several individual important sectors of Mexican industry, with particular attention paid to the two major foreign exchange earners of the steel and automotive industries.

Mexico has a well-developed steel industry, with output in 1986 of steel ingots 40% up on that of 1975 and output of steel sheet double the level of a decade earlier. In 1986 itself, output fell by several per cent under the impact of the recession on demand from the construction and capital goods industries. Even a sharp 85% increase in iron and steel exports—mainly to the US market—was unable to

TABLE 3.43   OUTPUT OF LEADING INDUSTRIAL PRODUCTS 1975–1985

	1975	1981	1982	1983	1984	1985
Steel ingots ('000 tonnes)	5176	7426	6910	6885	7272	7333
Corrugated steel rods ('000 tonnes)	691	1517	1372	1288	1380	1328
Steel sheet ('000 tonnes)	880	1644	1450	1472	1690	1805
Cement ('000 tonnes)	11503	17954	19091	17030	18348	18384
Beer (mn litres)	1968	2863	2803	2414	2559	2721
Soft drinks (mn litres)	n.a.	5006	5928	5432	4816	5428
Car tyres ('000)	3341	4878	5386	4962	5446	5530
Refrigerators ('000)	433	642	625	452	319	313
Washing machines ('000)	338	621	654	485	313	322
Tractors ('000)	10	19	16	11	10	12
Cars ('000)	262	369	324	214	245	285
Trucks ('000)	76	119	80	36	55	81

Source: Instituto Nacional de Estadística, Geografía e Informática

prevent output from contracting. Of total steel output, in 1985 the state iron and steel corporation, Sidermex, accounted for more than half. During 1986 the Sidermex Fundidora Monterrey subsidiary was closed, leaving the Sicartsa plant at Las Truchas and the Altos Hornos division in state hands. Much of the private sector steel industry is in the hands of Grupo Alfa, Mexico's largest non-public corporation and a group which has, like the country itself, suffered from high debts and the poor health of the domestic market. Nevertheless, despite the plight of the steel industry as a whole, the government recently approved further (430 billion pesos) investment to complete the construction of the Sicartsa II complex, which will add 1.5 million tonnes to Sidermex's (now slimmed down) capacity. The Sicartsa I complex is already highly export oriented, with around half of the plant's 1986 output of 863,000 tonnes of finished steel products being sold abroad in the United States, Europe, the Middle East and the Far East.

TABLE 3.44   THE IRON AND STEEL SECTOR 1980–1986

	1980	1981	1982	1983	1984	1985	1986p
Production ('000 tonnes)							
– steel	7156	7673	7056	6978	7560	7368	7170
– laminated products	5981	6280	7652	5491	6006	5953	5482
Exports (US$ mn)	71.5	64.0	112.4	318.5	377.7	239.1	443.1

Source: Banco de Mexico
Note: p – provisional

Over the past decade, the country has developed a major automotive industry, based primarily upon European and American designs and technology. The sector is an important cog in the world automotive industry, whereby engines and other parts are exported from Mexico to Europe and the United States. Not only has the closed nature of the Mexican vehicle market induced multinational manufacturers to locate plants in the country, but they have also (post 1982) been attracted by low labour costs and a favourable exchange rate. The year of peak historical output was 1981, when exports of built-up vehicles were tiny and the domestic market was expanding rapidly under boom conditions. In late 1982 the market and output both collapsed sharply, to recover over 1984–5 when production levels resumed their 1979–80 position. During 1986, however, the economic crisis and a sharp rise in interest rates caused the car and truck market in Mexico, as well as output, to fall by around 30%. The industry has, however, since 1982 been gearing up for increased export sales, which over 1982–6 in fact quadrupled—and the Mexican Government continues to have high hopes in this direction for the future.

Eleven companies are active in vehicle manufacturing in Mexico (twelve until 1986, when Renault pulled out). Chrysler, Ford, General Motors, Nissan and Volkswagen manufacture automobiles and vans, and Diesel Nacional, Fabricantes Autotransportores Mexicana, Kemworth Mexicana, Trailers de Monterrey, Victor Patron and Mexicana de Autobuses produce trucks and/or buses. The industry has also been beset by a proliferation of models which have proved uneconomic. Accordingly, from 1984 the government has passed legislation to reduce the total number of models produced and to boost possible economies of scale. As a result, companies have been restricted to producing three model groups in 1984, two in 1985 and 1986 and only one in 1987. Inauguarated on 14 November 1986, the new Ford plant at Hermosillo is the most recent showpiece of the Mexican automotive industry. Built at a cost of US$500 million, the plant has an installed capacity for 130,000 vehicles and covers 113 hectares. Using local content of 30% the works employs some 1600 persons and is an integral part of Ford's North-American manufacturing programme.

Dominated by PEMEX (the state-owned oil corporation Petroleos Mexicanos), the petrochemicals industry has expanded rapidly in importance, with output in 1986 approximately twice as substantial as in 1979/80. Clearly, the coming on-stream of the Mexican oil industry

TABLE 3.45   PRODUCTION AND EXPORTS OF MOTOR VEHICLES 1976–1986

('000)	1976	1977	1978	1979	1980	1981	1982	1983	1984	1985	1986p
Production											
Automobiles	213	188	243	280	303	355	301	207	245	297	215
Trucks and buses	112	93	142	164	187	242	172	78	113	162	112
TOTAL	325	281	384	444	490	597	473	285	358	459	327
Exports											
TOTAL	4	12	26	25	18	14	16	22	34	58	63

Source: Asociacion Mexicana de la Industría Automotriz
Note: p – provisional

provided an ideal opportunity for import substitution in this crucial sector, with output continuing to grow in 1986 despite a collapse in export sales in that year. Mexico is, however, still not self-sufficient in petrochemicals, with the trade deficit in this product area in 1986 running at US$295 million—admittedly 41% lower than in 1985. The value of petrochemical exports in 1986 collapsed, due chiefly to a sharp fall in the volume and value of ammonia sales. The Mexican industry now comprises well over 110 plants, including the major PEMEX La Cangreja complex in Veracruz which came on-stream in mid 1984.

TABLE 3.46   THE PETROCHEMICAL INDUSTRY 1979–1986

	1979	1980	1981	1982	1983	1984	1985	1986p
Production ('000 tonnes)	6345	7224	9160	10589	11265	11221	12402	13769
Exports ('000 tonnes)	750	755	812	873	806	576	339	188
Exports (US$ mn)	108	125	154	140	124	128	76	29

Source: PEMEX
Note: p – provisional

XVI   Transport and communications

Mexico's difficult terrain means that, over large parts of the country, air travel is the only practical means of transport, and the country has a large domestic network of internal air services. The country boasts around 50 airports, of which at least half are of international standard.

The national road network is similarly extensive, comprising around 250,000 kilometres, of which one-third is paved. At the end of 1986 there were an estimated 5.25 million cars and 2.25 million trucks in circulation, of which around half are to be found in the congested and smog-bound national capital.

Mexico's railways total almost 26,000 kilometres of track. Despite a substantial investment programme started in 1983, the system (which is state run) is in very poor shape, with antiquated track and rolling stock keeping journey times to an uncomfortable maximum.

Few of Mexico's rivers are navigable; the shipping sector is thus primarily coastal and marine. The merchant marine can carry only a few per cent of Mexico's foreign trade, and the country is still hampered by a paucity of good port facilities—although plans are in hand to remedy this (eventually) by development at Tampico, Mazatlan and Salinas Cruz, among other ports.

TABLE 3.47   TRANSPORT AND COMMUNICATIONS 1981–1985

	1981	1982	1983	1984	1985p
Paved roads (km)	68455	70234	70840	71631	72521
Railways (km)	20196	21291	25799	25840	25866
Airways (mn passengers)	20.7	29.7	31.6	31.8	33.4
International airports	32	34	32	32	32
Shipping ('000 tonnes)	95605	101994	101724	98331	97759
Telephones (mn units)	5.5	6.0	6.4	6.8	7.3
Radio stations (units)	864.0	867.0	873.0	882.0	887.0
TV stations (units)	180.0	284.0	405.0	407.0	429.0

Source: Agenda Estadística 1986/Instituto Nacional de Estadística, Geografía e Informática/SPP
Note: p – preliminary

XVII   Tourism

The tourism sector is a mainstay of Mexico's economy and constitutes a very important source of foreign currency. In 1984, 4.66 million foreign visitors arrived in Mexico (including the millions of short-stay frontier excursionists), a total which fell sharply during 1985 in the wake of the devastating September earthquake. During 1986, however, the number of arrivals picked up again to reach a provisionally estimated 4.6 million—with the depreciation of the peso and the World Cup largely responsible (although the football extravaganza attracted far fewer visitors than had been hoped). Only a few per cent of foreign arrivals are from Europe, with tourists predominantly Americans seeking one or two weeks' sun/beach/Latin culture.

In 1984, earnings from tourism reached US$1.95 billion, which fell sharply during 1985 to some US$1.73 billion. In 1986 the falling (despite an increase in tourist arrivals) peso receipts fell modestly to approximately US$1.8 billion. In 1986 tourism earnings approximated 1.3% of GDP and accounted for 10–11% of total export revenue (up on the 8–8.5% of 1984–5). In 1986, outgoings on the national international tourism account were provisionally estimated at US$620 million, with a surplus of more than US$1.17 billion being earned for the Mexican economy.

Mexico City, Acapulco, Cancun, Puerto Vallerta and Mazatlán are all major tourist destinations, attracting at least 300,000 tourists each in a 'normal' year. The national tourism infrastucture is constantly being upgraded, although the recessions of 1982–3 and more recently of 1986 have badly affected investment. The state organization Fonatur, mindful of the phenomenal success of Cancun, has been instrumental in directing investment (under way for some years now) to Los Cabos and Loreto in Baja California, to Ixtapa north of Acapulco and to Huatulco in Oaxaca. On the optimistic side perhaps, the National Tourism Plan of 1984–8 hopes to raise the total number of foreign visitor arrivals to Mexico to six million by the late 1980s—although shortcomings to be surmounted include wider promotion of Mexico as an international tourism destination and an improvement in cheap-rate air communications with Europe.

TABLE 3.48   TOURISM 1982–1986

	1982	1983	1984	1985	1986p
Number of tourists ('000)					
Inflow	3768	4749	4654	4207	4625
Outflow	2671	1971	2697	2731	2490
Revenue (US$ mn)	1405.9	1624.5	1952.7	1719.7	1791.7
Expenditure (US$ mn)	787.7	441.3	648.6	664.3	620.2
Balance (US$ mn)	618.2	1183.2	1304.1	1055.4	1171.5

Source: Informe Anual 1986/Banco de Mexico
Note: p – preliminary

TABLE 3.49   GEOGRAPHICAL ORIGIN OF TOURISM TO MEXICO 1982–1986

(%)	1982	1983	1984	1985	1986p
United States	84.8	86.2	84.5	84.2	84.2
Canada	3.1	3.6	4.0	4.6	5.3
Europe	5.2	3.8	4.6	3.5	3.2
Latin America	6.4	5.9	6.2	7.1	6.9
Others	0.5	0.5	0.7	0.6	0.4
TOTAL	100.0	100.0	100.0	100.0	100.0

Source: Banco de Mexico
Note: p – preliminary

CHAPTER FOUR
COSTA RICA

I Political structure

Costa Rica is unique in Central America, being the region's sole established democracy. Since 1948, when the army was ousted after a contested election, politics have been dominated by conservative and liberal groupings, currently organized as the United Social Christian Party (PUSC) and the National Liberation Party (PLN). The two parties have tended to alternate in power. However, in February 1986, the ruling party secured a second successive term for only the second time in the country's history, when Oscar Arias Sánchez became President, succeeding his PLN colleague, Luis Alberto Monge Alvarez.

Simultaneous elections to the country's 57-member legislative assembly gave the PLN an overall majority, although the PUSC increased its representation from 17 to 25 seats to deny the ruling party the two-thirds majority required for constitutional changes. Despite the ruling PLN's liberal ideology, the massive economic problems spawned by the country's US$4.1bn foreign debt—one of the highest per capita in Latin America—have obliged the last two governments to adopt a form of fiscal austerity more commonly associated with the conservatives.

While the country's democracy is more consolidated that that of any other state in Central America, Costa Rica's traditional foreign policy of neutrality has come under intense pressure since 1981, as a result of Washington's support of the contra rebels battling the Sandinista Government in Nicaragua. There have been several border incursions by Sandinista troops and by contras belonging to the independent rebel group led by Edén Pastora, and later by those belonging to the US-backed United National Opposition (UNO) group. The Costa Rican Government's apparent tacit support for these contra groups, particularly during the administration of Luis Alberto Monge, has become a major domestic and international issue. Diplomatic relations with Nicaragua were severed at one point, while Costa Rica itself has become gradually militarized. The country's Civil Guard has tripled in number to about 12,000, and recruits are now armed.

However, since 1986 the Arias Government has had some success in restoring the image of the country's neutrality, playing an active role in the Contadora group, improving relations with Nicaragua and even proposing a Costa Rican peace plan. However, the price has been a deterioration in the country's relations with the Reagan administration.

The foreign debt and delicate state of the economy have been the other major threats to the country's stability in recent years. Costa Rica has traditionally boasted one of the most developed social security systems in Latin America, and since the 1940s the national budget has always placed a heavy emphasis on provision of public services such as housing, education and health. However, within months of coming to power in 1986, Arias was forced to initiate another round of IMF austerity policies, which involved raising basic food prices, withholding salary rises to public workers and cutting the number of government employees by 3000.

II Demography

Costa Rica has an estimated population of 2.71 million, with an annual growth rate of about 2.5%. This gave the country a population density of just under 52.9 persons per square kilometre in 1985. The capital, San José, houses nearly 15% of the total population and is the only major conurbation in the country. The next largest towns are Puntarenas and Limón, but both cities are only about one-fifth of the size of the capital.

The population is predominantly of European stock, as a result of the very small number of indigenous inhabitants encountered when the Conquistadores settled the country. Today, the indigenous population numbers less than 0.7% of the total, with the only major ethnic minority being the blacks concentrated on the Atlantic coast.

As in the rest of Central America, there has been a radical shift to urban centres in recent years. In 1986, more than half the population lived in towns, compared to less than one-third 25 years before. The relatively young age of the populace and the austerity measures induced by the foreign debt burden have caused a substantial rise in unemployment, which has added to the urban drift.

III   Domestic economy

Costa Rica recorded stable economic growth of at least 5% per annum during the 1970s before a deterioration in the country's terms of trade and the increased burden of debt servicing saw GDP shrink 2.3% and an unprecedented 7.3% in 1981 and 1982 respectively. Indeed, President Luis Alberto Monge inherited an economy in disastrous shape when he acceded to power in 1982. Inflation was nearing 100%, the public sector deficit had reached more than 15% of GDP and the current account deficit was running at about 16.5% of GDP. The recession, and an almost complete absence of fresh investment, saw production plummet with a consequent increase in unemployment and social tension. Moreover, President Carazo's confrontational approach in talks with creditors, culminating in the unilateral suspension of interest payments in the final quarter of 1981, had made the country an international credit pariah.

Within weeks of taking power in May 1982, President Monge began talks with the IMF and instituted tough austerity measures that, although reducing inflation and the fiscal deficit, depressed growth still further that year. However, by 1983–4 the new policies had begun to bear fruit and the economy expanded 2.9% and 7.5% in successive years. Despite a slight slowdown in 1985, when GDP growth per capita contracted again, expansion has continued, with the economy registering growth of 3.2% in 1986.

TABLE 4.1   GDP GROWTH 1980–1986

	1980	1981	1982	1983	1984	1985	1986
GDP growth (%)	0.8	−2.3	−7.3	2.9	7.5	1.6	3.2
GDP growth per capita	−2.1	−4.8	−9.8	0.2	4.8	−0.8	0.4

Source: Ministry of Planning

However, there are doubts about the foundations of the recovery, which seems to be the result of a combination of favourable circumstances as much as sounder economic policies. High export prices for coffee and the fall in the price of oil played a major role in stimulating consumption in 1984 and 1986. There has also been a rise in public investment, which is unlikely to be maintained.

The contraction of the economy in 1982 combined with record

inflation of more than 90% that year, as the government introduced IMF measures that included eliminating subsidies and holding back wage rises. However, inflation fell away rapidly in 1983–4 to stabilize at about 14% in 1985 and 1986, although the administration has failed in its aim of reducing the level of price rises to single figures.

The key factor in economic policy since 1982 has been the International Monetary Fund (IMF), with whom the government has been obliged to negotiate standby facilities in 1982, 1985 and 1987. IMF demands have included the slashing of subsidies, the dismantling of protectionist barriers, steady devaluation of the colón to keep exports competitive, tax reform, the rationalization of the public section and the freezing of salaries. This has spawned some diversification of exports and a sharp drop in the fiscal deficit to 5.7% of GDP in 1986.

Since President Oscar Arias came to power, however, the government has adopted something of a low-key confrontation approach on the debt in an effort to win better terms from the IMF. Arias is determined to retain some of the social policies promised in the 1985 election campaign. From July 1986, the government declared a moratorium on principal due and started paying only 4% in interest payments.

Althouth this stance seemed to have helped Costa Rica to secure relatively favourable terms on a US$55m standby facility from the IMF in 1987, commitment to social schemes and subsidies has caused policy rifts in the cabinet. In March 1987, Central Bank president Eduardo Lizano offered his resignation on the grounds that he lacked presidential support for sound fiscal policies and the structural economic reforms backed by both the World Bank and the IMF. However, under pressure from key members of the cabinet, who feared damage to the country's credibility in debt talks, Lizano was reinstated and his arch rival, Agriculture Minister Alberto Esquivel, lost his job. The division over policy, however, will remain, those advocating the undiluted economic reform backed by the IMF still facing opposition from key cabinet members who have the President's sympathy.

The government's economic policies have combined with other favourable developments, such as the duty-free provisions of the Caribbean Basin Initiative (CBI), to stimulate foreign investment interest in Costa Rica. The country has a relatively sophisticated infrastructure, boasting the best telephone system and cheapest electricity rates in Central America, as well as the most skilled labour

TABLE 4.2   FOREIGN DEBT 1982–1986

(US$ mn)	1982	1983	1984	1985	1986
Public sector	2961	3407	3433	3584	3600
Private sector	536	441	500	500	400
TOTAL	3497	3848	3955	4084	4080
Rate of growth (%)	4.1	10.0	2.8	3.3	−2.1

Source: Ministry of Finance

force. A leading private sector investment group, Cinde (the Costa Rican Coalition for Development Initiatives), believes that tax exemptions on imported machinery and profits have played a major role in seeing more than 200 new foreign investment plants set up since 1983.

Further incentives, such as a lowering of corporation tax rates, are likely, but problems remain. The domestic market remains relatively depressed and is always vulnerable to the kind of austerity measures agreed with the IMF. Furthermore, foreign companies face problems in obtaining currency for imports, as well as profit and dividend remittances.

The budget deficit has proved the most contentious issue with the IMF since 1985, despite a steady fall to 5.8% of GDP in 1986. The government's agreed aim is to reduce this to 3% of GDP by 1988. Public spending will be cut and surpluses in autonomous institutions such as the Social Security Institute and the national refinery will be written into the national accounts.

But spending remains the government's major problem, given the country's extensive social security system and the current administration's pledges on expenditure. The 1986 budget was 44bn colónes, a 12.5% rise on the previous year's C39.1bn but a slight decline in real terms. Government revenues of C35.7bn in 1986 were supplemented by new bond issues worth a total of C5bn. However, the ease with which spending can get out of control was seen during the first half of 1986, when the budget deficit grew to C3600m, only marginally less than the C3977m figure registered for the whole of 1985.

IV   External position

In 1986, exports broke the US$1bn barrier for the first time in five years, running to an estimated US$1073m. The figure represents a US$112.2m increase on the US$962m worth of products exported in 1985, with coffee, bananas and beef, the country's three main agricultural exports, all rising. However, coffee producers have claimed that the government did not take full advantage of high prices last year, while the failure of International Coffee Organization (ICO) states to agree on quotas depressed average prices during 1987 to less than half their 1986 levels.

While Costa Rica's export performance will always be closely linked to the world prices of the key agricultural exports that account for 60% of export earnings, the government's efforts to stimulate non-traditional exports have enjoyed some success. Exports in this category rose 16% in 1986 to reach US$336m, about 30% of total earnings. Flowers, fruits and vegetables are the leading new exports.

TABLE 4.3   FOREIGN TRADE 1981–1985

(US$ mn)	1981	1982	1983	1984	1985
Exports (fob)	1008.1	870.4	882.4	1006.4	961.8
Coffee	240.7	236.9	230.1	261.8	310.1
Bananas	246.9	228.1	240.4	231.8	212.2
Beef	74.0	53.1	31.9	49.2	55.7
Sugar	43.1	16.6	23.9	31.6	9.5
Imports (cif)	1209	893	989	1090	
Raw materials	567	436	447	487	
Consumer goods	252	167	216	259	
Capital goods	258	167	136	169	
Fuels	75	87	100	86	

Source: Academía de Centroamérica

The collapse of Central American Common Market (CACM) commerce, which has shrunk to less than half its 1981 value of nearly US$1.2bn, has hit Costa Rica particularly hard. With one of the region's most diversified industrial bases, manufactured exports to El Salvador, Honduras, Panama and Nicaragua have traditionally been a major source of income. In 1986, exports to CACM states contracted a further 29.7%, slumping to only US$92m. This represents less than one third of the value of Costa Rica's trade with its neighbours in 1980, and commercial difficulties have been compounded by the fact that credits have not been serviced. Indeed, Costa Rica is owed more by CACM members than any other country in the group—a total of about US$340m.

The strength of the country's manufacturing base means that raw materials and capital goods account for nearly half Costa Rica's total imports. The value of imports has risen steadily since 1982, when the depth of the recession saw the bill for foreign goods fall by more than 25% to US$893m. In 1984, consumer goods accounted for 23.7% of total imports, with spending on capital goods running to US$169m and the oil bill falling 14% to US$86m.

Nearly 40% of all trade is with the United States, with Central America accounting for 17% of exports and 9.8% of imports in 1985. Imports from CACM states have fallen much more marginally than exports, dropping 12% to US$87m in 1985. West Germany is the country's only other major trading partner, taking 9.2% of exports and about 5% of imports in 1985.

The impact of the higher costs of Costa Rica's imports and depressed commodity prices has not been alleviated by the devaluations and export incentives of the last five years. The country has recorded trade deficits in each year since 1980, and foreign aid has become a critical factor in economic calculations.

TABLE 4.4   AGRICULTURAL PRODUCTION 1983–1985

('000 tonnes)	1983	1984	1985
Coffee	123	151	121
Bananas	1154	1161	1100
Sugar	2618	2936	2800
Rice	281	223	219
Maize	105	103	107
Beans	21	23	25
Beef	61	76	62

Source: FAO

Economic Support Funds from the United States quadrupled in 1983 to US$200m, to make the country the world's second largest recipient of US economic aid on a per capita basis. Indeed, economic assistance in each of the three years between 1983 and 1985 was equal to almost all US aid in the 1961–80 period. About 80% of the US aid dispersed in this period was in the form of Economic Support Funds (ESF), which are direct cash transfers to the Central Bank. Much of the money was then channelled to the private sector for the purchase of imported manufactured goods, raw materials and inputs. Although the rise was largely attributable to the debt payments crisis, USAID officials admitted that the increase in bilateral assistance was also designed to offset the perceived threat from the Sandinista Government in Nicaragua. The aid also lessened any resistance from the Costa Rican Government to the contras operating from national territory in their guerrilla war against the Sandinistas.

V   Structure of production

Agriculture is the basis of the economy, accounting for nearly 20% of total GDP in 1985. Coffee and bananas are the main export crops, earning US$522.2m, more than 50% of total earnings, in 1985, when coffee output was 121,000 tons and banana production was 1100 tons. Sugar has decreased in importance, as a result of low world prices and cuts in the US sugar quota. The crop earned only US$9.5m in 1985, less than one quarter of its value in 1981, although production has remained fairly steady at about 2.8m tons. Meat exports have also been hit by low prices, although the national herd has continued to expand.

A relatively large middle class and the country's traditional political stability have stimulated Costa Rica's manufacturing base which, along with that of Guatemala, is the most developed in the region. Although food processing remains the main activity, the country boasts textile, chemical, plastic and metal processing plants. However, manufacturing's contribution to GDP, traditionally about 20%, has shrunk in recent years as a result of the steep decline in regional trade. An increase in exports to other areas, particularly the United States, has not made up for the contraction in the regional market, while the value of exports has not balanced spending on the imported capital goods and raw materials essential to the manufacturing sector.

The mining industry is underdeveloped, despite known reserves of iron ore, bauxite, sulphur, manganese and both silver and gold. Only the precious metals are mined, with production of silver and gold estimated at 57 kilograms and 820 kilograms respectively in 1984, although smuggling may account for as much as 90% of production. Plans to exploit the bauxite deposits abandoned by the US multinational Alcoa have been scrapped in the face of low world prices, which have also hit the government's hopes of resurrecting interest in the country's oil deposits.

TABLE 4.5   STRUCTURE OF GDP 1980 AND 1985

(at 1984 prices)	1980		1985^e	
	US$ mn	%	US$ mn	%
Agriculture	762	18.0	843	19.6
Mining and manufacturing	930	22.0	948	22.0
Commerce	764	18.1	708	16.4
Financial services	511	12.1	562	13.0
Government	424	10.0	419	9.7
Transport and communications	297	7.0	308	7.2
Construction	264	6.2	199	4.6
Electricity, gas and water	99	2.3	141	3.3

Source: IDB
Note: e – estimate

The Mexican state oil monopoly PEMEX abandoned a two-year exploration and drilling programme in 1984 because of high costs. This has left Costa Rica dependent on imported fuels, the cost of which rose as high as US$100m in 1983. However, power for electricity generation now comes almost wholly from domestic sources such as the hydroelectric plant on Lake Arenal in Guanacaste province. The complex, inaugurated in 1979, has a total generating capacity of 1974 MW. Work has begun on a geothermal energy plant, while other unconventional sources of power are already making significant contributions to the national grid. Wood and bagasse (sugar-cane waste) already supply about one-quarter of the country's fuel for electricity generation, and cane alcohol could become an important source in the future.

Although the transport infrastructure is better than those in many other Central-American countries, less than one-fifth of the country's 30,000 kilometres of roads are paved. The main route through the country remains the north-south Pan-American Highway that links Costa Rica to Nicaragua and Panama. New road projects have been delayed or cancelled as a result of government austerity measures, although work on new port infrastructure at Caldera on the Pacific coast has gone ahead. As a result of the country's budget problems, the contribution of the transport and communications sector to overall GDP has grown only fractionally, being worth an estimated US$308m, or 7.2% of the total in 1985. This represents a substantial decline in real terms on the US$297m figure posted in 1980.

The railway network stretches through San José to link the Pacific and Atlantic ports of Puntarenas and Limón, with a branch line running into Panama, via Pandora. However, rolling stock and tracks are old and the lines are designed principally to transport freight, particularly bananas. The only international airport serves San José, being located 10 kilometres outside the capital at El Coco.

VI Standard of living, consumption

Costa Rica's traditionally high standard of living and consumption level has been hit by budget cuts and fluctuations in economic growth during the last seven years. Wage rises, particularly in the public sector, have consistently lagged behind the rate of inflation, while the elimination of subsidies on basic foodstuffs has caused big rises in the price of rice, beans, corn and flour. In 1987, the Arias administration agreed to halve the deficit of the National Production Council, which buys beans, rice and corn from farmers and sells them to consumers. This will mean the elimination of more price supports.

In 1986, the government altered the procedure for wage rise settlements in the private sector. Automatic bi-annual adjustments made with reference to an accepted price index were abolished and replaced by an annual review which will take place only when a broader price index shows a rise of 7% or more. Meanwhile, wages in the public sector have been frozen, and the number of civil servants will be cut back to 1984 levels by the end of the decade.

Lower real wages, higher prices and increased taxation have thus all hit consumption patterns since 1981. Although imports have risen steadily since the 25% slump in 1982, most of the increase has been in the form of inputs for the export sector. Imports of consumer goods in 1985 were no higher than the US$252m level registered in 1981. However, the consumer market is still richer per head in population than in any other country in Central America. There are more than 40 passenger cars and 85 television sets in use per 1000 inhabitants in Costa Rica—double the levels registered in Honduras and Nicaragua.

Costa Rica's welfare state, the foundations of which were laid in the 1940s and 1950s, has bequeathed the country a literacy rate of more than 90%, an average life expectancy of 72 years and an infant mortality rate of only 19.3 per 1000 live births—the lowest in Latin America after Cuba. Moreover, school enrolment is more than 80%, and there is one doctor for every 1523 inhabitants. Education is free up to 16 years of age, and 80% of the population qualify for free health care.

However, social spending has come under severe pressure as a result of IMF-induced austerity measures and shortfalls in government revenue in recent years. While health spending was increased about 7% in real terms to 1550m colónes, and the education budget rose 6.4% to 8387m colónes in the 1986 budget, the shortfall in coffee earnings and higher oil prices meant that neither ministry received their full allocation. Further cuts are inevitable, while the country's housing shortage, estimated at more than 150,000 units, will be accentuated by the severe curtailment of President Arias' ambitious plans to build 80,000 houses before 1990.

CHAPTER FIVE
EL SALVADOR

I Introduction

The Republic of El Salvador is a densely populated country of 21,400 sq km whose once high population growth rate has diminished in recent years. It is the smallest and most industrialized of the Central-American republics, with all its available land put to use and with a coffee-based economy for whose cultivation the rich porous volcanic soil in the highlands (often farmed beyond 1200m in altitude) is ideal. Most of the cultivable land was owned by a group of rich land-owners known as the '14 families', but since 1980 about 20% has been redistributed to peasants under a land reform programme.

The greater part of El Salvador is volcanic upland, two rows of volcanoes crossing the country from west to east, with lowlands to the north and south and a short Pacific coastline. It is bordered by Guatemala to the west and Honduras to the north and east. The climate is semi-tropical and temperature varies with altitude, the average being 25°C (23°C in San Salvador, the capital, at 680m). There is one rainy season from May to October, but a spell of continuous rainy weather sometimes occurs over a period of days or weeks in December and March.

II Government and political structure

El Salvador was under sustained military rule from 1932 to 1979, when a coup resulted in the installation of a civilian-military junta, amid turbulent events marked by the emergence of a revolutionary guerrilla movement, killings by both right and left, arrests and disappearances, and labour unrest. Events spiralled downwards into a civil war, which ever since has drained the country's resources and severely disrupted business and production. In December 1980 Sr José Napoleón Duarte of the Christian Democratic Party (PDC) was appointed President of El Salvador at the head of a civilian-dominated junta under pressure from the United States, which proceeded to increase aid to the country substantially. In 1982 a newly-elected Constituent Assembly appointed a centrist non-party figure, Dr Alvaro Magaña, to take over from the junta as interim head of state in the run-up to presidential elections, which were eventually held in two rounds in March and May 1984. Sr Duarte was elected President for a five-year term, and in 1985 a 60-member unicameral Legislative Assembly was elected for a three-year term, dominated by the PDC which won 54 per cent of the vote and 33 seats.

Although peace talks took place in 1984 and again in April 1986 between the government and the guerrilla movement—the Farabundo Martí National Liberation Front (FMLN), estimated to be about 6000 strong—little of substance emerged from the talks. The government requirement that the FMLN should cease fire and join in the political process remains at odds with the FMLN's assertion that they will do this only if they are allowed to participate in a provisional government of national consensus which would open a 'national dialogue' and call free elections. Heavy military operations designed to destroy major strongholds, plus a strategy of isolating the FMLN and keeping it on the move, have had the effect of forcing it to change its own tactics towards an increasing reliance on economic sabotage of roads, coffee-processing plants and power installations, with occasional acts of terrorism. The FMLN adapted swiftly to the new tactics and is reported to be active in almost all the 14 provinces. Thus there seems little prospect of an early end to the war, of which the Salvadorean people appear to be weary. Labour activism was renewed in 1985, and in February 1986 thousands of demonstrators marched through the capital calling for a withdrawal of austerity measures imposed the previous month, and for renewed peace talks with FMLN.

Popular support for Sr Duarte appears to be waning, and his standing with the military was not helped when in October 1985, in return for the release of his daughter who had been kidnapped by the FMLN, he allowed 22 political prisoners to be released and about 100 wounded guerrillas to leave the country. However, no effective alternative to the PDC has emerged, since the right, embodied in the National Reconciliation Party (PCN) and the Nationalist Republican Alliance (Arena), is split and the left is out of the running.

III   Demographic structure

The great majority of the people are *mestizos*, small percentages being pure Indian or of unmixed white ancestry. The last census took place in 1971, but at mid 1985, according to national projections, the population numbered 5.2 million, 45% of whom were under 15 and less than 5% over 60. The population of the San Salvador area rose between 1971 and 1985 by 72% to 1.27 million (445,000 of these, according to 1983 figures, in the capital itself). Some 42% of the population live in the towns, and the greatest concentrations of population other than in San Salvador are in Sonsonate and Cuscatlán, the smallest being in Chalatenango. Overall population density at mid 1985 was 248 per sq km (compared with 169 per sq km in 1971).

Since the beginning of the civil war there has been a major displacement of the population, and this worsened as large-scale army operations intensified in 1986 to clear out guerrilla strongholds. Over 600,000 people are estimated to have been displaced; some 21,000 are in refugee camps in Honduras (the vast majority of whom arrived in 1981, and half of whom are under 14). Direct US aid to refugees amounts to US$40m a year, and other foreign refugee aid to US$20m a year. Due to the flight of population, the growth rate is estimated by the government to have diminished from an average of 2.8% between 1971 and 1985 to about 1.5%.

IV   Domestic economy

The problems El Salvador is experiencing are reflected in the state of the economy. Over one-quarter of the government budget goes on defence-related spending (compared with less than one-quarter on health and education combined). The cost of the war between 1979 and 1984 was estimated at US$1.2bn without taking into account factors such as flight of capital and loss of production and investment, and since then the cost has risen due to economic sabotage. Complete bankruptcy has been avoided and some growth maintained largely due to massive US aid (which in 1985 amounted to over US$300m), Inter-American Development Bank loans, Canadian and European capital assistance, and US export financing of US$95m in short- and medium-term credits through the Export-Import Bank. Between the beginning of 1980 and the beginning of 1985 an estimated US$1.7bn was transferred to the Salvadorean government from the US Treasury in Economic Support Funds (or cash transfers), of which 30% was in direct aid for the war, 44% in aid indirectly related to the war, and 25.5% for 'reform and development' (including agrarian, judicial and government reform) and commercial food aid.

The external debt totalled US$2bn at the end of 1985, and debt servicing for that year was equivalent to 43% of the country's export earnings. Interest payments on the debt were largely responsible for the increase in the current account deficit to US$117m in 1984 and to US$370m in 1985, compared with US$86.4m in 1983. The overall balance of payments improved slightly in 1985 to a US$40m surplus.

In January 1986 the government imposed an austerity package to stabilize the economy and stimulate growth. Inflation had increased from over 11% in 1984 to 22% in 1985; the unemployment rate was 36%, but even higher—over 50%—if the underemployed were taken into account; and GDP had grown only 1.6% (less than the 2% projected, and only marginally more than the rate of 1.5% registered in 1984). Real per capita income had fallen in 1985 to about 67% of its 1978 level. The budget deficit improved slightly, from 6.2% of GDP in 1984 to 5.5% in 1985, and the private sector grew by 9.1%, but public sector investment contracted by 11.1%.

In the austerity package the colón was devalued by 50% against the dollar and the two-tier exchange rate for the colón was abolished and a rate of 5 colónes per dollar fixed for all transactions. Under the dual system, an artificially low rate of C2.5 per dollar had been applied to coffee exports and to subsidize imports such as wheat, edible oil and fertilizers, and a parallel rate applied elsewhere, pegged at various values (from C4 to C4.85 per dollar in 1985). The price of dollars on the black market varied from C5 to C8.

To help reduce the budget deficit, a 15% tax was introduced on coffee exports. Price controls were extended to cover more basic items, and prices were frozen temporarily on certain essential items. Commercial interest rates were raised, and imports of non-essential goods were banned for one year. The industrial minimum wage and public sector salaries were increased by 10 to 15%, and increases were also recommended for the public sector. However, such wage rises were unable to compensate for the sharp rise in inflation in 1986.

V External trade position

El Salvador has had a trade deficit since 1981. This has steadily deteriorated to a low of US$304m in 1985. The value of exports totalled US$726m in 1984 and US$709m in 1985, while imports (mainly consumer goods, raw materials and intermediate products) rose from US$977m in 1984 to US$1013m in 1985. Exports to countries in the Central American Common Market fell by 20% due to exchange rate difficulties and payments problems.

VI Agriculture

Agriculture is the dominant sector in the economy, accounting for 25% of GDP, employing 40% of the workforce and contributing two-thirds of total exports. Coffee and cotton are the main export crops, with sugar cane increasing in importance. However, the destruction of plantations by guerrillas and the disruption of main roads has not only caused a sharp drop in the amount of coffee harvested and processed (to 2.5m quintales in the 1984–5 season, 40% lower than in 1979–80, and to 2.2m quintales in 1985–6), but has also deterred investment in new coffee bushes. About half of the farmland in the main agricultural district in the east of the country is reported to be fallow. Additional factors in the decline of coffee cultivation are, according to coffee growers, the nationalization of coffee exports and the effects of the 1980 land reforms.

The agricultural sector grew by only 1.2% in 1984 and in 1985 declined by 2.4%, partly because of bad weather. The declining production of cotton and coffee can be attributed to low domestic prices for coffee and low world prices for cotton, plus guerrilla disruption. Foreign exchange earnings from coffee exports (which normally accounted for over 50% of total export earnings) declined from US$675m in 1979 to US$408m in 1983, but earnings from the 1984–5 harvest rose to US$450m and, in spite of a smaller harvest in 1985–6, remained high due to the sharp rise of the price of coffee on the world market.

Cotton cultivation also underwent a serious decline, due to reduced output and to marketing problems. While 1.35m quintales were produced in 1980, this dropped to 886,000 in 1983 and to

627,000 quintales in 1984; revenue from cotton exports fell from US$56m in 1983 to under US$10m in 1984, the lowest for many years. In 1985, which saw a disastrous cotton harvest, stocks of cotton from 1984 were sold off in the expectation that declining prices on the world market would persist, and this accounted for the increased revenue from cotton exports in 1985.

On the other hand, the area of sugar cane under cultivation has been expanded and yields have improved. The 1984 harvest produced 3.4m tonnes of cane (13% more than in 1983), and 1984 sugar production accordingly increased by 4.5%. However, low sugar prices on the world market plus the imposition of US import quotas meant that the value of sugar exports fell by more than one-quarter in 1984, and suggest a poor outlook for sugar exports.

VII   Industry

El Salvador has a highly developed industrial sector, accounting for 17.5% of GDP, which diversified to export outside Central America in the aftermath of the 1969 war with Honduras, when it lost not only the Honduran market but also the right of passage of its goods through Honduras to Costa Rica and Nicaragua. The major export markets for Salvadorean goods are the United States (exports being worth US$413m in 1985), West Germany, Guatemala and Japan. Food processing, textiles, leather, pharmaceuticals, oil products and machinery are among the main industries, frozen shrimps are a leading export, and other goods manufactured for the export market include computer components, automobile parts, light fixtures, television sets and clothing.

Industrial production has been affected in recent years by the war and the economic recession, the low purchasing power of the population, and problems in neighbouring countries. Lack of foreign exchange has hindered the procurement of raw materials. Production of food, tobacco and textiles, accounting in 1982 for 72% of total industrial production, has undergone a 19% reduction. However, a 1.8% rise in industrial growth was registered in 1984 after several years of decline, and the state investment programme for 1984–5 foresaw the promotion of production and export potential and the improvement of financial structure through special credits.

The construction sector expanded by 12% in 1985, compared with a decline of 5.7% in 1984, and the total area constructed was almost double that of 1984.

TABLE 5.1   GDP BY SECTOR 1984

(US$ mn)	
Agriculture	917
Mining and quarries	7
Manufacturing industry	696
Construction	149
Electricity, water, sewerage	111
Transport, warehousing and communications	193
Commerce	1086
Financial	169
Housing	243
Government services	476
Other	363

Source: Banco Central de Reserva

TABLE 5.2   BALANCE OF TRADE 1982–1985

(US$ mn)	1982	1983	1984	1985[e]
Exports	699	735	726	709
Coffee	406	408	449	447
Cotton	46	56	9	29
Sugar	16	40	26	23
Shrimp	21	15	20	13
Imports	857	892	977	1013
(Crude oil	134	127	131	—)
Balance	−158	−157	−251	−304

Source: Banco Central de Reserva/Euromonitor
Note: [e] estimates

TABLE 5.3   MAJOR MANUFACTURED GOODS 1982–1984

(US$ mn)	1982	1983	1984p
Foodstuffs	526	591	668
Oil products	217	239	276
Beverages	108	121	136
Textiles	83	91	116
Chemical products	87	97	107
Clothing and footwear	83	93	106
Tobacco	36	43	48
Leather products	26	32	35

Source: Banco Central de Reserva
Note: p – provisional

TABLE 5.4   BALANCE OF TRADE WITH CENTRAL-AMERICAN
COUNTRIES 1977–1983

(CA$ '000)	1977	1978	1979	1980	1981	1982	1983
Exports (fob)	211653	233569	266601	295796	206484	174229	168101
Imports (cif)	210836	239948	256958	320362	304833	260850	233598
Balance	+817	−6379	+9643	−24566	−98349	−86621	−65497

Source: Dirección General de Estadística y Censos/Banco Central de Reserva/
national statistics

TABLE 5.5   NATIONAL STATISTICS 1983

Public expenditure	
Military	US$150m
Arms imports	US$ 40m
Education	US$ 35m
Health	US$ 53m
Foreign economic aid	US$300m
Human resources	
Armed forces	42000
Physicians	1800
Teachers	20000

Source: UN

TABLE 5.6 PRINCIPAL EXPORT MARKETS 1980–1984

(US$ mn)	1980	1981	1982	1983	1984p
USA	442	206	248	285	215
Guatemala	174	141	132	123	117
West Germany	149	263	205	140	128
Japan	43	38	23	37	32
Costa Rica	67	34	22	22	27
Nicaragua	55	30	17	15	5
Honduras	–	1	4	8	8
Others	144	84	48	105	229

Source: Banco Central de Reserva
Note: p – provisional

TABLE 5.7 IMPORTS BY COUNTRY OF ORIGIN 1980–1984

(US$ mn)	1980	1981	1982	1983	1984p
Guatemala	254	247	210	172	187
USA	194	250	233	289	325
Costa Rica	55	47	36	43	47
West Germany	24	37	40	36	43
Japan	38	33	27	31	42
Others	386	361	304	316	321

Source: Banco Central de Reserva
Note: p – provisional

TABLE 5.8 DISTRIBUTION OF POPULATION BY PROVINCE 1985

	Population	Density per sq km
Ahuachapán	257900	208
Cabañas	173300	157
Cuscatlán	214100	270
Chalatenango	226800	112
La Libertad	430600	260
La Paz	260100	212
La Unión	328200	158
Morazán	200600	138
San Miguel	467100	224
San Salvador	1266200	1429
San Vicente	209900	177
Santa Ana	449800	222
Sonsonate	353400	288
Usulután	407700	191

Source: West German Federal Statistical Office

CHAPTER SIX
GUATEMALA

I Political structure

Guatemala returned to civilian rule in January 1986 after more than 30 years of military-dominated government. Vinicio Cerezo Arévalo won an overwhelming mandate in a two-round presidential election in 1985, widely viewed as the first fraud-free poll since a decade of reformist government was ended in 1954 by a CIA-backed military coup. Cerezo's Christian Democrats also have a majority in Congress, but in reality the country's democracy remains very fragile, with much power still in the hands of the military. Cerezo has never hidden his acceptance of the fact that radical efforts to tackle the country's socio-political problems would provoke military intervention and the President has deliberately played down expectations. In 1986, he estimated that he held only 30% of total political power.

The major opposition party is the Union of the National Centre (UCN), whose presidential candidate, Jorge Carpio Nicolle, was beaten by Cerezo by a 2:1 majority in the second round of the election in December. Other parties represented in Congress include the Democratic Party of National Co-operation (PDCN), the ultra-right National Liberation Movement (MLN), the Democratic Institutional Party (PID) and the only left-of-centre group which fielded a presidential candidate in the election, the Democratic Socialist Party (PSD). However, the opposition is generally fragmented and personality-based.

Most of the country's problems are a legacy of the generals' period in power. Although the number of disappearances and political murders has fallen, the human rights situation remains poor. The government is under constant pressure from the Grupo de Apoyo Mutuo (GAM), a 1000-member pressure group consisting of relatives of the disappeared who are demanding a full inquiry into the fate of their family members. While international human rights groups such as Amnesty International and Americas Watch have identified G-2, the army's intelligence corps, as the hub of the security forces' death squad operation, a ruthless counter-insurgency drive in the Indian highlands of the country has failed to wipe out four guerrilla groups still fighting the government. Meanwhile, the unions, which have seen their leaders systematically killed off over the past two decades, have begun to take advantage of the limited democratic opening under Cerezo to demand higher wages and improved working conditions.

However, pressure from the right and the military is even more of a problem for Cerezo. Land reform and higher taxation, universally identified as the country's two most urgent necessities, have been ruled out by the right-wing parties and the omnipotent business group, the Co-ordinating Committee of Agricultural, Commercial, Industrial and Financial Associations (CACIF).

With little room for manoeuvre at home, Cerezo has set about repairing the image of Guatemala abroad. He has enjoyed considerable success in reducing the country's international isolation, and has begun to play a leading role in efforts to secure peace in the region. However, even here he has come under pressure, particularly from Washington, which is seeking an end to his 'active neutrality' policy and whole-hearted condemnation of Sandinista Nicaragua.

II Demography

In mid 1984, Guatemala's population was estimated at 8.16 million, but the annual average growth rate is high—more than 3% per annum in the countryside and about 2.8% per annum in the urban areas. More than 15% of the total population is concentrated in Guatemala City, the capital, while another 830,000 live in the department of Guatemala which surrounds the city. The capital houses more than ten times the number of residents found in the next largest conurbations, Escuintla and Quezaltenango, but there has been a considerable urban drift as a result of the high birth rates and intense pressure on land in the countryside.

More than 45% of the population is ethnically indigenous, descendants of the Mayan Indians subdued by the Conquistadores. They speak one of 23 different Indian languages and are confined mostly to the mountainous zones in the north and west where the agricultural land is poorest and most unworkable. About 40% of the population are *ladinos* of mixed blood, while about 10% consider themselves white, mostly of European stock. There are significant numbers of blacks on the Atlantic coast around Puerto Barrios, and about 2% of the population are of oriental origin, mostly Chinese and Lebanese.

Life expectancy is 58 years, and the death rate had fallen to 10 per 1000 in 1983. Although the infant mortality rate has been reduced, it is still more than double the national average in the rural areas, running to about 85 per 1000 live births. Population density was put at 75 per square kilometre in mid 1984, while the high birth rates and relatively low life expectancy means that an estimated 40% of the population are 18 years of age or less.

III   Domestic economy

Real Gross Domestic Product is estimated to have contracted 1% in 1986, the same as in 1985, following falls of 3.5% and 2.7% in 1982 and 1983 respectively. There was a marginal increase of 0.6% in 1984. With the population growing at about 3% per annum, GDP per capita has fallen steadily for the past five years. The economic stagnation and contraction of recent years contrasts sharply with growth that averaged 5% per annum during the 1960s and 1970s. The principal reason for the turnaround has been a deterioration of the country's terms of trade, but this has been compounded by steadily mounting debt payments, economic mismanagement during the last two periods of military rule, and a substantial fall-off in investment. The depletion of the country's foreign exchange reserves in 1984–5 saw inflation soar to an annualized 45% at one point, while the national currency, on a par with the US dollar for decades, plunged to 25% of its official value on the black market. Foreign credits and investment slowed to a trickle in the face of widespread human rights abuses and a raging civil war.

Since strong opposition had forced the military government of General Oscar Mejia Victores to cancel plans to cut subsidies and increase taxes, the Cerezo Government's first task was to introduce some form of financial stabilization package to halt the economic slide. The progress unveiled in 1986 introduced a three-tier exchange rate for the local currency, effectively devaluing the quetzal, and a sliding scale of taxation on basic agricultural exports. Tariff reforms and new forms of indirect taxation were also introduced to boost government income. Interest rates were raised to operate in a new band between 11 and 14%.

These measures have enjoyed some success, but other favourable economic developments have played an important part. The first of these was an improvement in the country's trading terms. The import bill in 1986 fell to about US$950m, compared to nearly US$1.1bn in 1985, largely as a result of a fall in purchasing power and the decline in the price of oil. The rise in the price of coffee saw export earnings from the country's leading agricultural crop rise 11% to US$501.3m, while sugar and banana revenue also improved. Invisibles have also played a major part. Income from tourism tripled in 1986 to US$40m, while foreign credits have flowed in again as a result of the improvement in the human rights situation and Cerezo's success in promoting his civilian government. The President's European tour yielded US$300m in commitments, one-third of which will be in direct grants, while US economic assistance rose to US$114m in 1986.

The main achievements of the stabilization programme can be seen in falling inflation, improved foreign exchange reserves and the stabilization of the exchange rate at about Q2.50:US$1. Inflation fell to an estimated 25% in 1986, despite the effective devaluation of the national currency. The main factor here has been the slowdown in the growth of the money supply, down to 17% in 1986 compared to 56.3% in 1985. Foreign exchange reserves, meanwhile, rose 20% to reach US$362m in 1986—their highest level since 1980.

But the critics emphasize that the stabilization has been achieved only at the cost of another fall in GDP growth and a big slump in consumption. Wage increases averaged only 11% in 1986. This represented the sixth successive year in which purchasing power has fallen, adding to the pressure for both economic expansion and substantial salary increases.

The key to economic growth will be finding the means to increase government spending. Most of the pressure for salary rises has come from the more powerful public sector unions, while economic expansion remains heavily dependent on state investment in the face of continued caution from the private sector. In 1984, private sector investment was the equivalent of only 5.8% of GDP, barely one-third of the level posted in 1978.

The government's principal problem remains the private sector's virulent opposition to any increase in direct taxation. Tax revenue in Guatemala is already the lowest in Latin America, representing just 5.3% of GDP in 1984. Moreover, indirect taxes provide more than 80% of total takings. Another modest tax reform proposal, calling for higher income tax rates and a wealth tax, was shelved in late 1986 in the face of more opposition from the business sector. Meanwhile, the Q2.55bn budget approved in November 1986 projects a Q830m deficit, and the government's revenue shortfall problem has been intensified by over-optimistic projections from the new export tax.

The fiscal deficit can deteriorate only if export earnings fall and imports rise as a result of the new stability in the exchange rate. Debt servicing payments, accounting for more than 20% of total spending in 1987, are due to increase, while a comprehensive rescheduling seems out of the question unless the government can force a rise in taxation. Failure to reduce the fiscal deficit was a major cause of the collapse of talks with the IMF in August 1984.

IV   External sector

Guatemala is critically dependent on the sale of primary agricultural commodities, which account for up to 70% of all export revenue. Traditional exports are coffee, cotton, sugar and bananas, but during the 1980s there has been some diversification with cardamom, sesame seed, meat and various fruits and vegetables becoming increasingly important. In 1986, non-traditional exports earned US$131m.

TABLE 6.1   FOREIGN TRADE 1982–1986

(US$ mn)	1982	1983	1984	1985	1986
Imports					
Consumer goods	284.4	235.3	242.7	224.9	n.a.
Raw materials	475.8	461.7	507.8	474.4	n.a.
Fuel	300.8	254.9	300.1	267.7	n.a.
Capital goods	242.9	115.4	133.0	153.8	n.a.
Building materials	77.3	59.9	56.3	50.4	n.a.
Exports					
Coffee	358.9	351.0	365.5	451.5	501.3
Cotton	79.5	50.2	75.8	73.1	28.2
Sugar	26.5	126.8	71.3	46.4	51.7
Bananas	110.6	70.8	60.8	70.9	73.4
Meat	15.3	15.0	15.0	10.0	5.3

Source: Banco de Guatemala

Dependence on traditional exports left the economy perilously exposed when world commodity prices slumped and the cost of oil soared during the early 1980s. Between 1980 and 1985, the real prices of the country's leading exports fell 35% and earnings tumbled from US$1.56bn in 1980 to US$1.06bn in 1985. Imports peaked in 1981 at US$1.67bn, when the trade deficit reached a record US$419.9bn. By 1985, however, this was down to a more manageable US$113m, although the only year this decade when the country recorded a surplus was 1983.

The situation would have been even worse if the country's oil industry had not been able to soften the impact of high fuel prices in the 1982–4 period. Although Guatemalan oil production never fulfilled its anticipated potential, production peaked in the critical years of 1982 and 1983, when output of 2.29 million and 2.55 million barrels respectively kept import costs down. Exports of oil also earned US$46.1m and US$60m respectively in these years, to help alleviate the trade deficit.

TABLE 6.4   OIL PRODUCTION, EXPORTS AND IMPORTS 1981–1985

	1981	**1982**	**1983**	**1984**	**1985**
Production ('000 barrels)	1493	2292	2549	1715	935
Exports ('000 barrels)	662	1546	2206	1248	456
Value of exports (US$ mn)	22.1	46.1	60.0	34.0	11.7
Value of imports (US$ mn)	378.4	303.0	256.6	303.1	278.0

Source: Ministry of Energy and Mines

The United States accounts for about one-third of Guatemala's exports and imports, but the most dramatic change in the direction of trade in recent years has been the decline in sales to neighbouring states in the Central American Common Market (CACM). Contracting markets, severe foreign exchange shortages and trading disputes saw CACM trade slump during 1985 to less than half its 1980 levels. Guatemala, with the most developed manufacturing sector in the region, has been particularly badly hit. CACM trade was down from US$397.2m in 1981 to US$236.7m in 1985.

Official government policy is to stimulate traditional exports while encouraging diversification. However, industrialists complain that the government's strategy is contradictory, given the special levy imposed on exports and the long delays in processing licences for imports that are often essential to manufacturing processes. There have also been bitter disputes over the activities of the international trade monitoring group, the Société Général de Surveillance (SGS), which the government contracted in an effort to halt under- and over-invoicing, which was said to be costing the country up to one-third of the value of its annual trade.

In the 1970s, the inflow of foreign currency hit record highs as coffee prices soared, the government began to borrow heavily, and aid flowed into the country after an earthquake, which claimed more than 22,000 victims, in 1976. However, these trends were completely reversed in the early 1980s. Commodity prices slumped, aid dried up and foreign exchange reserves plummeted to only US$112m in 1982, barely one-quarter of the level recorded two years earlier. By September 1985, the government had had to suspend final-quarter principal payments on five medium-term loans totalling US$105.6m as a result of the critical shortage of foreign exchange.

However, there is some truth in the administration's assertion that the country's debt is manageable if a comprehensive rescheduling accord can be reached. Guatemala's main problem is the bunching of payments on total foreign obligations estimated at US$2.8bn by end 1986. Despite arrears on commercial debt, significant progress has been made on renegotiating bilateral obligations, in particular nearly US$200m-worth of loans with the Venezuelan Investment Fund, the Banco de Mexico, the Trade Finance Corporation and the Banco de Santander.

But a larger-scale IMF-backed rescheduling is seen as inevitable. The country failed to meet its US$615.8m obligations in 1986 and carried over arrears of US$60m from 1985. With payments scheduled to rise until 1989, debt servicing is unlikely to fall below 40% of the total value of goods and services until 1990, according to the IMF. Rising budget deficits mean that the government is borrowing more, with a loan package totalling US$287m from 18 banks and agencies being contracted in 1986. More than 90% of the country's debt is owed by the public sector. The total has built up rapidly from less than US$550m in 1980 to nearly US$2.6bn by 1986. The poor credit-worthiness of the country throughout much of the 1980s has also ensured that much of the debt was incurred on particularly harsh terms, with high rates of interest and low maturity periods.

V Structure of production

Agriculture remains the most important sector of the economy, accounting for about a quarter of overall GDP and employing nearly two-thirds of the workforce. While coffee, sugar, cotton and bananas remain the most important crops, there has been considerable diversification in recent years into non-traditional vegetables and fruit. However, a private sector plan to boost non-traditional agricultural earnings to US$500m by 1990 is wildly ambitious. Rice, maize, wheat, sorghum and beans are cultivated for domestic consumption, but demand has begun to outpace output in some sectors during the last five years.

TABLE 6.3   AGRICULTURAL PRODUCTION 1981–1985

('000 tons)	1981	1982	1983	1984	1985
Coffee	173	159	153	140	171
Bananas	650	655	675	680	n.a.
Cotton	114	71	48	59	66
Sugar	444	550	563	533	545
Beans	81	84	89	90	111
Maize	997	1100	1046	1038	1080
Beef	95	75	63	64	n.a.

Source: United Nations Economic Commission on Latin America

Guatemala's manufacturing base is the most developed in Central America, having diversified from the traditional food and drink processing that sprung up around the agricultural sector in the 1970s. The sector now includes all kinds of textile plants, a steel factory, a petrochemical plant, and even a munitions factory and vehicle-assembly plant. Construction material outlets were boosted by the 1976 earthquake, and the country boasts several plants making or assembling a range of consumer goods. Much of the original manufacturing investment in the country was spawned by the increase in CACM trade in the 1970s, and the corresponding fall in intra-regional business and the drop in purchasing power have depressed the Guatemalan manufacturing sector and slowed its diversification. By 1985, its contribution to overall GDP had dropped to 15.7%.

Mining output has plummeted in the last seven years, and the sector's contribution to total GDP halved between 1980 and 1985. Production at the country's largest operation, a copper mine in Alta Verapaz, slowed as prices fell, while the Canadian company Eximbal closed a nickel mine in Huehuetenango in 1980 after only three years of production. The country has known deposits of lead, iron, silver and barite in addition to nickel and copper.

Production of oil rose substantially in the early 1980s, but output has declined as a result of lower prices, the inaccessibility of most of the country's reserves and the high sulphurous content of Guatemalan crude. Production peaked in 1983 and by 1986 had fallen by more than two-thirds. Despite government optimism, output seems certain to remain low. Several large multinationals, including Texaco and Elf Aquitaine, have now withdrawn from the country.

TABLE 6.2   GDP BY SECTOR 1980 AND 1985

(constant 1958 prices)	1980		1985	
	US$ mn	% of total	US$ mn	% of total
Agriculture	772.0	24.9	753.7	25.5
Commerce	839.1	27.0	739.3	25.0
Manufacturing	517.3	16.7	462.3	15.6
Financial services	244.7	7.9	268.3	9.0
Transport and communications	215.8	7.0	205.4	6.9
Public administration	163.0	5.2	192.2	6.5
Construction	97.9	3.1	53.0	1.8
Electricity, water and gas	53.2	1.7	56.4	1.9
Mining	14.8	0.5	6.5	0.2
Other services	163.0	5.2	192.2	6.5

Source: Consejo Monetario Centroamericano, Boletín Estadístico

One compensation has been increased exploitation of the country's hydroelectric potential. The 90 MW Aguacapa hydroelectric project came on-stream in 1981, while the long-delayed Chixoy scheme, with a generating capacity of more than 300 MW, finally started production in 1987. Various other smaller hydroelectric and goethermal projects are planned.

The contribution of the transport sector to total GDP remained static during the first five years of the decade, but value fell by nearly 20% as government investment was cut back. Large areas of the country in the north and west remain unconnected to the capital, although a major northern transval route through the provinces of Alta Verapaz and El Quiche is being completed. There is only one international airport, while rail and port infrastructure is generally poor.

VI Consumption

High inflation and substantial real ralls in wages have drastically eroded purchasing power in Guatemala since 1981. Per capita growth has been falling since the late 1970s, but the sharpest drops in purchasing power came in 1984–5 when inflation hit more than 45%, while the foreign exchange crisis forced the government to cut subsidies on basic foods and transport. In 1986 this process continued, with wages rising an average of 11% while prices increased more than 30%. Both private and public consumption have fallen in real terms since the beginning of the decade, and in 1986 imports were 30% down on the US$1.56bn level registered in 1981. Consumer goods have held up best, falling only 21% from the level recorded in 1980 to US$224.9m in 1985. The market for capital goods slumped by nearly 40% in the same five-year period.

TABLE 6.5 CONSUMPTION INDICATORS 1980–1985

	1980	1981	1982	1983	1984	1985
Private consumption (mn quetzals)	6217	7022	7151	7501	7885	9250
Government consumption (mn quetzals)	627	680	676	688	716	760
Consumer price index (December to December)	9.1	8.7	−2.0	8.4	5.2	31.5
Nominal wages and salaries	10.9	31.2	6.2	−2.9	2.7	7.0

Source: IMF/international financial statistics/UN Economic Commission for Latin America

A substantial upturn in demand is impossible until the country develops a more diversified economy and workers see real wage rises. Although statistically one of the richest markets in Central America, consumer potential is radically reduced by the marginalization of large sections of the population, particularly the indigenous people. Dependent on subsistence agriculture in isolated parts of the country, many Guatemalans remain virtually outside the money economy. The standard of living of the vast majority has been hit by substantial real cuts in health and education spending during the last five years. Military expenditure has absorbed huge slices of the national budget as a result of the counter-insurgency drive, while the government's failure to increase revenue through higher taxation has had a direct impact on the already inadequate social services.

CHAPTER SEVEN
HONDURAS

I Political structure

Plagued by 400 armed rebellions and more than 120 governments
since independence, Honduran history is one of chronic political
instability. However, after elections in 1981, the process of
democratic consolidation took a big step forward in January 1986
when President Roberto Suazo Cordoba became the first modern
head of state to hand over power to an elected successor. In reality,
however, the military retain a large measure of power, and the
influence of the United States, traditionally based on the critical
economic role of the American banana companies, has increased
with the use of the country as a base for up to 30,000 Nicaraguan
contras.

One demonstration of the military's determination to retain
ultimate power came in November 1982 with the passage of
amendments to the constitution promulgated earlier that year. The
military increased its political influence by securing congressional
support for a measure that made the head of the armed forces, rather
than the president, Commander-in-Chief.

Despite the relative political stability of the eighties, there have
been numerous coup plots and some blatant manipulation of a
constitution that has often been found wanting. There are also
frequent and ever-changing divisions within the two main political
groups, the National Party (PN) and the Liberal Party (PL). Indeed,
with the personality-based factions in both groups unable to agree on
an individual party candidate for the 1985 presidential poll, a total of
seven PN and PL nominees appeared on the ballot papers.

José Azcona Hoya was only declared President on the basis of an
electoral reform measure awarding victory to the party receiving the
most votes. Inevitably, the manner of his accession bequeathed the
new President a very divided party. Moreover, the Liberals backing
Azcona secured only 46 of the 134 congressional seats and decided on
a coalition with the opposition Nationalists rather than reconciliation
with the President's Liberal rival, Oscar Mejia Arellano, who
secured 18 seats. The Nationalists were awarded two key portfolios in

the cabinet share-out, but the ruling majority has always been inherently unstable with personalities counting for more than policies. Moreover, at the beginning of 1987, PN leader Rafael Leonardo Callejas announced the end of the pact with the PL. There is little in terms of ideological differences between the two major parties. The National Party has traditionally been more right wing, but both Suazo and Azcona are on the right wing of their own Liberal group. Rafael Leonardo Callejas, the major PN candidate in the 1985 poll, did put forward a more pro-business programme than his opponents, but the only consistent political strategies put forward came from minority candidates. One of these was Carlos Roberto Reina, a dissident Liberal leading the Molider tendency who stood on a platform opposing the increased militarization of the country and the stepped-up role of the United States. He was joined in this by Hernan Corrales Padilla of the Christian Democrats (DC) and Enrique Aguilar Cerrato of the Innovation and Unity Party (Pinu), both of which won two seats in Congress.

The tiny guerrilla groups that have sprung up periodically over the last 20 years have always been wiped out at an early stage and the country has generally avoided the intense civil conflict of its neighbours. However, many Hondurans see the presence of the contras and US troops as a threat to their relative stability. Border raids by the Sandinistas and political killings, often linked to the presence of the contras, have increased markedly in the last two years. So far, the country's politicians have swallowed their nationalist pride in exchange for big increases in US aid, but constant manoeuvrings within the Honduran armed forces are an indication of the struggle over the US role.

II Demography

The population of Honduras was estimated at 4.49 million in 1986 and the country has one of the highest population growth rates in Latin America—more than 3% per annum in 1985. There has been a remarkable shift to the urban centres in recent years, with 40% of the total population now living in towns, the biggest of which are the capital Tegucigalpa with an estimated population of 830,000, San Pedro Sula (373,000), La Ceiba (64,200) and Choluteca, El Progreso and Puerto Cortes with about 54,000 inhabitants each.

Some 50.4% of the population were female at the last census in 1984, with life expectancy put at 58 years. Infant mortality rates remain high, averaging between 80 and 95 deaths per 1000 live births between 1980 and 1985. The high population growth rate of recent years means that more than 50% of the population are believed to be 20 years of age or less. The literacy level has increased only marginally in recent years and was put at 64% in 1985. About 85% of the population are considered *mestizo*, with the most significant minority groups being indigenous Amerindian (9%), black (2%), white (2%) and Chinese and Oriental (1%).

Honduras has a much smaller population yet bigger surface area (43,277 square miles) than that of its neighbours El Salvador and Guatemala. This has spared the country the intense pressure on land that has been a significant contributing factor to the civil wars in other Central-American states. Density per square kilometre was 36.5 in mid 1983. However, the drift to the cities as industrialization has continued is causing social problems more typical of the remainder of Central America. The numbers coming on to the job market have risen steadily, and despite growth in each of the three years since 1984, GDP per capita has contracted steadily since the beginning of the decade.

III   Domestic economy

Economic growth in 1986 was estimated at 2–2.5% of GDP. This represented the third successive year of growth after expansions of 2.8% and 2.6% in 1984 and 1985. However, population growth of more than 3% per annum continues to outstrip the economy's performance, and per capita GDP fell for the sixth successive year in 1986. Moreover, with income per head averaging less than US$700 a year, Honduras is already the second-poorest country on the Latin-American continent.

Since the return to democratic rule in 1981, the objectives of government policy have changed little. Export-led growth, reduction of the fiscal and external deficits and the control of inflation have been the principal aims. This has seen the government introduce austerity measures under the terms of a US$150m IMF standby credit agreement concluded in October 1982. The accord was abandoned in November 1983, the Fund claiming that the government had failed to meet economic targets. Subsequent talks have foundered on Tegucigalpa's refusal to devalue, although a series of tax increases and spending cuts cleared the way for increased levels of US aid in 1984. Such funds have since helped support fiscal deficits, which have persistently remained above 6% of GDP. Although there has been some progress in budgetary terms, the economy remains critically dependent on the world price of the country's main exports, namely bananas and coffee, which together account for more than 50% of total export earnings.

Efforts to diversify into non-traditional agricultural products and to expand the country's industrial base to take advantage of duty-free provisions in schemes like the Caribbean Basin Initiative have met with strictly limited success. In reality, it is the increased flows of foreign aid, particularly from the United States, that have come to the rescue of an essentially stagnant economy and allowed the government to resist pressure from both the IMF and Washington for a devaluation of the lempira.

However, the overvalued exchange rate has contributed to low inflation in recent years. In 1986, retail prices rose by only 5.5% and food prices rose by less than 3%. In 1984 and 1985, the consumer price index rose only 4.7% and 3.4% respectively, and three years ago food prices actually fell. The government's anti-inflationary policies have helped keep inflation in single figures since 1980, but wage settlements have also been low. This reflects the low level of unionization and unemployment of about 25%, made worse by recent budget cuts. The legal minimum wage ranged between US$2.65 and US$3.55 per day in 1985, while underemployment, particularly prevalent among the seasonally-employed, agricultural workforce, is estimated at up to 50%.

TABLE 7.1   HONDURAN LABOUR FORCE BY SECTOR 1984

(%)	
Agriculture	53.3
Manufacturing	13.3
Trade	9.66
Construction	4.34
Transport and communications	3.99
Finance	0.91
Mining	0.38
Others	13.8

Source: Banco Central de Honduras

Agriculture still employs more than half the workforce, although the proportion has been falling as the numbers working in construction, manufacturing and the service sectors have increased. The total workforce was estimated at 1.4m in 1986, with 38.2% employed in construction, manufacturing and the service industries and 52.7% working on the land.

Private foreign investment has been strictly limited in recent years, despite several measures designed to increase the attraction of the country since 1982. Most capital spending has come from the government and multilateral agencies such as the World Bank, EEC and IDB. The biggest projects have concentrated on improving the country's infrastructure or the agro-export sector, with the most ambitious projects being two hydroelectric schemes at El Cajon and Yojoa on the Lindo River. The first of these, with an eventual generating capacity of 292 MW, has already made a significant dent in the country's oil import bill.

The government declared its intention of stimulating further export investment in 1987 with a strategy that places particular emphasis on attracting direct foreign interest and rationalizing the public sector. New credit lines for both non-traditional and traditional exports have been opened and a stock exchange is planned to give firms access to more finance. Profits generated from exports shipped to destinations outside the Central American Common Market are already exonerated from income tax for ten years, while non-traditional exports are exempt from payment of the 1% export tax. The government has also opened a trade-free zone in Puerto Cortes in a redoubled effort to take full advantage of the duty-free privileges offered by the Caribbean Basin Initiative (CBI) and the Generalized System of Preferences (GSP).

IV   External position

Coffee and bananas account for more than 50% of the country's export earnings, with wood, timber, sugar, cotton and shellfish making up most of the remainder. The country's principal imports are raw materials, fuels, capital goods and consumer products, with oil remaining the single largest purchase.

The heavy dependence on primary agricultural exports and raw material imports means that the country's trade balance is highly susceptible to the fluctuations of world prices for key commodities such as coffee, bananas and oil. High coffee prices, which averaged US$2 per pound, and the slump in the oil market, helped close the trade deficit to about US$180m in 1986. However, the fall in the cost of oil imports was offset by a big increase in the purchases of foreign consumer goods, leaving the import bill virtually unchanged at an estimated US$957m.

TABLE 7.2 IMPORTS AND EXPORTS 1982–1985

(US$ mn)	1982	1983	1984	1985
Imports				
Raw materials	238.7	289.1	301.1	327.8
Fuels	170.1	163.8	179.6	163.6
Capital goods	114.8	125.5	168.1	183.0
Durable consumer goods	55.3	50.1	69.5	75.6
Non—durable consumer goods	103.8	122.6	128.7	140.1
Building materials	25.9	48.8	39.2	42.7
Exports				
Bananas	218.3	203.2	232.8	288.1
Coffee	153.1	151.2	169.1	185.2
Wood	44.7	40.4	34.9	32.6
Sugar	21.6	27.8	25.6	21.4
Beef	33.9	31.4	21.2	21.7

Source: Consejo Monetario Centroamericano/Boletín Estadístico

However, by 1987 coffee had slumped to little more than half its average price the previous year in the wake of the failure of the International Coffee Organization (ICO) to agree on a quota system. Sugar, traditionally the country's third most important export commodity, has also been dealt a severe blow by another round of cuts in US import quotas. The country will suffer direct losses of US$7.5m as a result of the cuts.

Export revenue will also have suffered from a crisis in the mining industry. Rosario Resources, which operates the country's most important mine at El Mochito in Santa Barbara province and has a virtual monopoly of gold and silver exports, has announced its intention to withdraw from the country. The mine is for sale, and closure would cost the country about US$60m in lost exports and leave the 2000-strong workforce redundant.

The government's efforts to stimulate foreign trade were boosted by the declaration of 1987 as the Year of Exports. The strategy is backed by US$23.5m in USAID funds, which will be used to establish fresh export credit lines and finance marketing and promotional activities. However, besides variation in prices, exporters face the problem of the uncompetitive exchange rate, poor infrastructure and the low level of industrialization. Moreover, increased production of manufactured goods for export involves increased imports of both raw materials and the capital plant and equipment needed for production.

The USA is easily the country's most important trading partner, accounting for 53% of exports and 42% of imports in 1985. West Germany remains the country's second-most important market, while imports from Brazil and Japan have increased noticeably in recent years. However, Honduras remains the Cinderella of the Central American Common Market, the underdevelopment of its manufacturing base ensuring that the country runs substantial trade deficits with its more developed neighbours, particularly Guatemala, El Salvador and Costa Rica. Meanwhile, the huge contraction in intra-regional trade has dashed the government's hopes of finding new markets close to home.

The deficits on the trade and current accounts have only been possible because of significant inflows of capital from abroad, mostly in the form of aid from Washington and the multilateral agencies. Bilateral assistance from the United States rose from US$45m in 1981 to more than US$247.5m in 1984, although nearly one-third of this was military aid. In 1986, economic assistance was US$104.5m.

TABLE 7.3   US AID 1981–1987

(US$ mn)	Economic	Military	Total
1981	36.1	8.9	45.0
1982	78.1	31.3	109.4
1983	102.7	37.3	140.0
1984	168.7	78.5	247.5
1985	139.0	62.5	201.5
1986	104.5	80.6	185.1
1987			187.8

Source: Banco Central de Honduras

Despite such inflows, the country's foreign debt has mounted and now exceeds US$3bn. Much of this was contracted on concessional terms, and interest payments of US$279m represent a relatively low debt-service ratio in comparison to other Latin-American debtors. However, the government was forced to start talks on the rescheduling of over US$200m of government-guaranteed commercial debt in 1985, but was unable to meet creditor demands, largely as a result of the failure to reach agreement with the IMF.

The drop in oil prices and the increase in coffee earnings afforded Honduras some breathing space in 1986, but the radical deterioration in the country's terms of trade, combined with the stabilization of inflows from Washington, are expected to force Tegucigalpa back to the negotiating table shortly. The problem of capital inflows has been exacerbated by the almost complete drying up of foreign investment. Indeed, private investment dropped 65% between 1981 and 1985, according to the IDB, while capital flight in the five years to end 1984 exceeded US$800m, despite the government's efforts to attract foreign interest in the country.

V Structure of production

Despite diversification efforts, the country's structure of production has changed little in the last decade. Agriculture remains the basis of the economy, accounting for 27.5% of GDP, more than 50% of the workforce and three-quarters of export earnings. Although manufacturing grew at an average of nearly 6% per annum during the 1970s, its contribution to total GDP has in fact contracted, shrinking from 14.6% in 1980 to 12.4% in 1985. Both mining and construction have remained relatively stable in recent years, contributing 1.8% and 3.6% respectively to total GDP in 1985. In the same year, commerce represented 10.9% of total output, banking and financial services 10%, transport and communications 6% and government 4.4%.

Agricultural production is based on export crops, mostly bananas, coffee, sugar and cotton. Domestic production revolves around the cultivation of beans, maize, rice, plantains and sorghum. Traditionally, the country has been self-sufficient in such crops, although there have always been supply and storage problems. However, production by smallholders in the border areas, where domestic harvests are concentrated, has been hit by contra activity in recent years, and imports of beans and staple grains have increased.

Forestry and fishing have become increasingly important export sectors in recent years. Forests cover more than 4m hectares of the country, with hardwoods being cut near the coast and pinewood

TABLE 7.4   GDP BY SECTOR 1980 AND 1985

(constant 1966 prices)	1980		1985	
	US$ mn	% of total	US$ mn	% of total
Agriculture	269	26.1	299	27.5
Manufacturing	155	14.6	134	12.4
Commerce	113	10.9	118	10.9
Banking, finance and insurance	107	10.4	108	10.0
Transport and communications	61	6.0	65	6.0
Government	43	4.2	48	4.4
Construction	38	3.7	39	3.6
Mining	20	1.9	20	1.8
Electricity, gas and water	17	1.7	19	1.8
	212	20.5	229	21.2

Source: Consejo Monetario Centroamericano

production concentrated in the interior. Lumber exports were worth US$32.6m in 1985 and the country boasts more than 100 sawmills and two pulp plants. Seafood production is concentrated on the most profitable exports, namely shrimps and lobster, which in 1984 were worth US$39m.

The manufacturing industry is based on agro-sector processing, in particular meat packing, sugar and coffee processing, paper and pulp production and the canning of various types of fruits and vegetables. Most of these companies are owned by foreign interests, in particular Castle & Cooke and United Brands. There is also a limited amount of textile and furniture production, while other forms of assembly-type operations, including electronics, have been stimulated by the establishment of the free-trade zone in Puerto Cortes.

TABLE 7.5   PRODUCTION OF PRINCIPAL PRODUCTS 1982–1985

	1982	1983	1984	1985
Soft drinks ('000 bottles)	444674	489606	516093	477577
Beer ('000 bottles)	110546	131160	142398	132204
Cigarettes ('000 packets)	114072	101221	106936	115594
Matches ('000 packets)	60470	64081	60016	65166
Cloth ('000 yards)	10042	14311	16206	13883
Cement ('000 bags)	6528	11422	12569	8177
Wheat flour ('000 quintals)	1208	1359	1388	1475
Rum ('000 litres)	1871	1705	1716	1533

Source: Banco Central de Honduras

The country boasts considerable reserves of iron ore, coal, tin pitchblende and antimony, but production is confined to lead, zinc, silver and gold. Output has been hit by low world prices, while the future of production itself now seems under threat given the intention of Rosario Resources to withdraw from the country. Wood remains the principal source of domestic energy, although over 70% of total energy requirements have traditionally come from oil. However, this proportion is set to fall as energy from two hydroelectric plants comes on-stream. Several leading oil companies, including Texaco, Exxon and Cambridge Resources Corporation, have explored extensively for oil both on- and offshore. As yet no commercially viable deposits have been discovered, and the recent fall in the price of crude seems certain to deter further interest. Texaco continues to operate a small refinery at Puerto Cortes.

Although there has been some development of the country's infrastructure in recent years, the contribution of the transport and communications subsector to total GDP grew by only US$4m in the five years to 1985, and roads, railways, airports and ports remain inadequate, according to many exporters. Puerto Cortes on the Caribbean coast is the country's largest shipment terminal, handling more than half Honduras' total exports. There are three international airports in Tegucigalpa, San Pedro, Sula and La Ceiba. The road system remains poor, with the size of the country, its mountainous and jungled terrain and scattered communities adding to the problem. Barely 12% of the 17,200 kilometres of road are asphalted.

Financial services are geared to local industry, particularly the export sector, and remain fairly basic. The largest banks are the Bank of Montreal and Citibank, although other foreign finance houses work through local subsidiaries. Chase Manhattan owns 25% of Honduras' largest commercial bank, Banco Atlantida.

VI Standard of living

The standard of living in Honduras is low, even by Central-American standards. The high birth rate, poor, or at best uncertain, economic prospects, and chronic underdevelopment seem certain to ensure that there will be little in the way of tangible improvement in the provision of health care or education in the near future. Indeed, the standard of social services seems to have fallen in the last five years, while an IMF agreement, regarded as increasingly inevitable by many economic analysts, could force deep public spending cuts in 1987–8.

large sections of the population are marginalized, either in the dirt-poor countryside or the slums that have sprung up around the urban centres over the last decade. The average per capita income of about US$680 per head per annum in 1984 makes the country second only to Haiti in the league table of poverty in the Western Hemisphere. In the countryside, however, most peasant incomes are less than US$400 per annum, and the higher than average population growth here, combined with the failure of the government's land reform programme, means that the situation is deteriorating rapidly.

TABLE 7.6   CONSUMPTION INDICATORS 1982–1985

	1982	1983	1984	1985
Private consumption (mn lempiras)	4074	4326	4527	4797
Government consumption (mn lempiras)	805	889	960	1052
Imports (mn lempiras)	1629	1810	2116	2289
Consumer Price Index (% change)	9.0	8.3	4.7	3.4
Real wages (% change)	−0.5	−7.7	−4.5	−3.3

Source: IMF/international financial statistics/UN Economic Commission for Latin America

Despite the low level of inflation in recent years, the wages of most Hondurans have failed to keep pace with the rise in the Consumer Price Index since 1980. Average purchasing power has therefore slumped, most notably in 1983 when inflation of 8.3% saw real wages drop 7.7%. The growth in non-oil imports in 1986 is largely accounted for by an increase in spending on capital goods. There was also a rise in demand from a relatively small section of the population who benefited from the boom in coffee earnings and the overvaluation of the lempira against the US dollar.

CHAPTER EIGHT
NICARAGUA

I Introduction

Nicaragua is the largest and most sparsely populated of the Central-American republics, with a land area of 128,000 sq km, relatively little of which is put to economic use. Honduras is to the north and Costa Rica to the south. The country can be broadly divided into three geographical regions. In the centre is a large mountainous triangular area. In the east is a wide belt of densely forested lowland with a sparsely inhabited Atlantic (Caribbean) coastline, peopled by Indians and by Creoles (the descendants of colonies of Jamaicans settled by the British at the towns of Bluefields and San Juan del Norte in the 18th century). From the Gulf of Fonseca on the Pacific, a belt of lowland runs diagonally south-eastwards across the isthmus through two huge lakes—Lake Managua (1042 sq km) and Lake Nicaragua (8200 sq km)—to the Atlantic. All the large towns and 90% of the population are in this Pacific plains region, including Managua, the capital, which lies on the shores of Lake Managua. There is much volcanic activity at the north-western end of the lowland (from Lake Nicaragua to the Gulf of Fonseca). In Lake Nicaragua itself there are three volcanoes; another, Momotombo, lies on the northern shore of Lake Managua; and north-west of Momotombo is a row of over 20 volcanoes, some of them active. Managua was completely destroyed by earthquakes in 1931 and in December 1972.

The climate of Nicaragua is tropical and very humid, and there is a rainy season (winter) from June to November.

II Government and political structure

In 1978-9 a brief but devastating civil war fought by the Sandinista National Liberation Front (FSLN) brought to an end nearly 50 years of rule by the Somoza family. Named after General Augusto César Sandino, who led opposition to the US military occupation of

Nicaragua before being assassinated in 1934, the FSLN, now generally known as the Sandinistas, has held power since 1979. Until 1984 executive authority was held by a junta of national reconstruction co-ordinated by Commander Daniel Ortega, but in November 1984 Commander Ortega was elected President, with 67% of the vote. A new National Assembly was also elected (to replace the old Council of State), in which the FSLN won 61 of the 96 seats. Other seats were won by the Democratic Conservative Party (14), the Independent Liberal Party (9), the Popular Social Christian Party (6), and two each by the Communist Party, the Socialist Party and the Marxist-Leninist Popular Action Movement. The main opposition grouping, the Nicaraguan Democratic Co-ordination, abstained in the elections, even though certain restrictions on civil liberties which had been imposed under a state of emergency in 1982 were lifted beforehand.

Certain of the articles of a new constitution, which came into force in January 1987 to replace the old pre-1979 constitution, were immediately suspended when President Ortega reimposed a state of emergency.

The government of Nicaragua faces enormous problems. Internally, it is opposed by the private sector for its economic policies, particularly that of extending the state's role in the economy. It also faces demands for autonomy from the Miskito communities on the east coast, and progress is being made towards this end. However, US hostility on the grounds of Nicaragua's political direction, the support which Nicaragua allegedly channels to left-wing guerrillas in El Salvador, and the threat which it claims Nicaragua poses to the region as a whole because of its build-up of arms, has turned Nicaragua into a beleaguered nation. President Reagan warned Americans in March 1986 that 'using Nicaragua as a base, the Soviets and Cubans can become the dominant power in the crucial corridor between North and South America', from where they would be in a position to 'threaten the Panama Canal, interdict our vital Caribbean sea lanes, and ultimately move against Mexico'. The major external threat to Nicaragua comes from the US-backed counter-revolutionary guerrillas, or contras, armed opponents of the regime most of whom are former National Guardsmen. The two main contra organizations are the Nicaraguan Democratic Force (FDN), operating in the north and east close to and from Honduras and since mid 1985 in the Boaco-Chontales region, and the Revolutionary Democratic Alliance (ARDE), operating in the south from Costa Rica. Millions of dollars worth of aid was supplied to the contras by the United States in 1981–4, and a further package of US$100m was approved by Congress for 1987; however, this was held up when it emerged in late 1986 that proceeds from secret US sales of arms to Iran had been transferred to the contras, sparking off a major scandal in the US administration. In June 1986, in response to complaints filed by Nicaragua, the International Court of Justice at The Hague ruled that the United States had acted in breach of international law by intervening in the affairs of another state, and urged it to make reparations to Nicaragua for the damage caused.

There seems little prospect of a negotiated end to the conflict, despite the efforts since 1983 of the Contadora Group consisting of Venezuela, Panama, Colombia and Mexico and, since late 1985, of a Contadora 'support group' of Peru, Argentina, Brazil and Uruguay. The army numbers 50,000, in addition to which there are reserves and militias, and 200,000 of the population are said to be armed. Almost 20,000 Nicaraguans have been killed and another 20,000 wounded up to the beginning of 1987, and damages had amounted to US$2.8bn, equivalent to the national budget for a year.

Apart from supporting the Sandinista Government's opponents militarily and financially, the US administration in May 1985 imposed a trade embargo against Nicaragua. The impact of the embargo is mainly political, since Nicaragua had been diversifying its trade since 1981 when the United States suspended all its aid, and the embargo is not supported by the Western industrialized nations.

In spite of its problems, Nicaragua has achieved considerable progress in the social sphere. Illiteracy, affecting half the adult population in 1979, had been reduced by the end of 1981 to 13% as the result of a major campaign, and the infant mortality rate declined between 1979 and 1984 from 121 to 80 per 1000 live births. Over 15% of the 1987 budget was destined for education and 14% for health, although both these sectors face continued disruption by fighting. Between 1979, when a land reform programme was initiated, and 1986, some 30% of cultivable land was distributed to 600,000 people—half the rural population—and another 100,000 people were due to benefit in 1987. Over half the land distributed belonged to large estates and the rest was abandoned land already being worked by the people, who were given title to the land.

III Demographic structure

Three-quarters of the people of Nicaragua are Spanish-speaking *mestizos* concentrated on the Pacific plains and in the cities; the remainder are English-speaking Creoles and Miskito, and Sumo and Rama Indians speaking indigenous languages, who are concentrated on the east coast. The last census took place in 1971 and established a population of 1.88 million and a population density of 16 per sq km; according to mid-1985 estimates, the population numbered 3.22 million and population growth between 1971 and mid 1985 averaged 3.9% per annum, the highest in Latin America. Overall population density is about 27 per sq km, but varies widely between the densely populated Pacific region (61 per sq km), the centre and the north (17 per sq km), and the east coast (4 per sq km). One-third of the population lives in the capital, and over half in the towns; half of the population is under 15.

Nicaragua's 16 departments were reorganized in 1982 into 16 regions and (on the eastern side of the country) three special zones, each with its own local administration:

i) Estelí, Madriz, Nueva Segovia (pop. 320,000)—coffee and basic grains.
ii) León and Chinandega (pop. 500,000)—cotton, sugar cane, bananas, sesame, sorghum, corn, minerals (gold and silver). The chief port, Corinto, is in this region, and some industrial development is in progress.
iii) Managua (pop. 1,000,000)—industrially the most developed area.
iv) Granada, Masaya, Carazo, Rivas (pop. 500,000)—coffee, sugar cane, basic grains, sorghum, beef, vegetables. There is fishing and some industrial development.
v) Boaco and Chontales (pop. 340,000)—beef, basic grains, minerals.

Special Zone I: the north of Zelaya department on the east coast (pop. 100,000)—forestry, minerals and fishing.
Special Zone II: the south of Zelaya department (pop. 70,000)—fishing, sugar cane, coconut, basic grains.
Special Zone III: department of Río San Juan (pop. 35,000)—beef, basic grains.

IV   Domestic economy

The Sandinista Government inherited a devastated economy at the
end of a civil war whose cost in terms of damage and disruption to
agriculture, industry and trade was estimated at US$1.3bn. Progress
towards reconstruction has inevitably been slow. The continuing
need to sustain military activities within the country drains the
economy, and half of the budget goes on defence. There is little
public investment in infrastructure. The supply of basic goods is
disrupted by the state of emergency, manpower is diverted and
market supply vehicles commandeered, and student and international volunteers help to bring in the coffee harvest.

1984 proved to be Nicaragua's worst year since 1979. GDP was
estimated to have declined 1.4%, compared with over 3% growth in
1983, and has not yet regained its pre-1979 level; per capita GDP fell
by 4.7% over 1980–4. Formal unemployment in 1984 was 20% and in
1985 was 22%. The current account deficit had risen to US$530m by
the end of 1984, and capital expenditure had fallen from 35% of the
budget in 1983 to 15.7% in 1985. The budget deficit amounted to 17%
of GDP in 1986. In spite of rescheduling agreed over 1981–4, debt
servicing obligations in 1986 were equivalent to more than one-
quarter of export earnings (twice the 1985 level) on a 1985 debt of
US$5.6bn, and in mid 1985 creditor banks agreed to defer for one
year the US$295m overdue, out of an estimated total debt to the
banks of US$1.3bn.

The cost of a basic market basket of goods for a middle-income
family was estimated to have increased by over 110% in 1984, and by
over 80% for a low-income family, while for the period January–
November 1985 the increase for a comparable basket of goods was
over 160% for the better-off family and over 300% for the poorer
family. Prices are controlled for rice, beans, sugar, cooking oil, soap
and salt (all of which are rationed), but these and other goods are
available at higher prices on the free market. Workers on fixed
salaries have access to goods at subsidized prices as a means of
encouraging them to stay in vital sectors.

In February 1985 a severe austerity programme was adopted by the
government. Expenditure was cut, food subsidies were suspended,
public transport and petrol prices rose sharply, new salary structures
were introduced and the minimum wage was raised by between 13
and 47% depending on sector. The two-tier exchange rate for the

córdoba which had been in force since 1979 (C10 per dollar at the official rate and C28 per dollar at the parallel rate, compared with up to C600 per dollar on the black market) was replaced by a five-tier rate (respectively 10, 20, 28, 40 and 50 córdobas per dollar), and an official parallel market rate was established at the same time to attract dollars from the black market (on which the price for a dollar was over C900 by the end of 1985).

In early 1986 the córdoba underwent a further devaluation, and the five-tier rate was replaced. The new exchange rate for most transactions was fixed at C70 per dollar, although the official rate for payment of debt servicing obligations contracted prior to February 1985 remained at C10 per dollar. Transactions such as shipping, insurance, or remittance of profits to foreign workers would use a rate of C70 per dollar for half of the value and the official free-market or parallel rate for the other half. Exporters of non-traditional products such as seafood and handicrafts could retain and exchange 25% of their dollar earnings at the parallel rate.

In March 1986, in an attempt to reduce the budget deficit, the government increased taxes on cigarettes, soft drinks and alcohol and announced price increases of up to 150% on a variety of food and household items. Petrol prices were increased by 45%, but bus fares in Managua were frozen. A 50% increase in salaries was announced, subsequent to an earlier increase in January which had raised the salaries of the highest paid by over 100% and those of the lowest paid by only 58% in a move to redress the erosion of pay differentials. Wages were frozen from March onwards.

TABLE 8.1   ECONOMIC INDICATORS 1980–1985

	1980	1981	1982	1983	1984	1985
GDP (US$ mn 1980)	2219	2338	2319	2422	2388	2325
% change	4.9	5.4	−0.8	4.4	−1.4	−2.6
GDP per capita (US$ 1980)	801	817	784	792	755	710
% change	1.5	2.1	−4.0	1.0	−4.7	−5.9
Population (mn)	2.77	2.86	2.95	3.05	3.16	3.17
Unemployment (%)	18.3	14.8	14.5	18.9	21.4	22.2
Budget deficit as % of GDP	8.8	11.8	13.0	27.7	24.8	22.2

Source: CEPAL/Instituto Nacional de Estadísticas y Censos

V Structure of production

Agriculture is the main sector of the economy, employing 40% of the workforce and contributing 25% directly to GDP, but more indirectly in that many agricultural products such as timber, tobacco, sugar cane and rubber are converted into industrial products locally. Food crops grown are beans, maize, rice and sorghum, but food production is at present unable to keep up with demand, and emphasis is now on the production of food for a 'survival economy' rather than on expanding and diversifying export crops.

Coffee and cotton together make up 60% of total exports; other major exports are beef and sugar, and seafood is fished off the east coast. The war against the contras has contributed to the stagnation of the agricultural sector, and output in 1984 dropped by over 5%. Coffee and cotton production has fallen, while cotton and sugar have suffered from bad weather and from falling world prices (although Nicaragua has preferential price agreements with the Comecon countries for coffee and sugar).

Coffee accounts for almost half of export earnings, but the 1985–6 harvest was the lowest on record. The estimates for the 1986–7 harvest were more optimistic. Nicaragua failed to benefit in full from high world coffee prices in 1986 due to the fact that one-third of its crop had already been sold on the futures market.

Cotton production had been falling due to low world prices, a shortage of foreign exchange, a severe drought in 1986 in cotton-growing areas, and the spread of pests, but production in 1986 showed a recovery. The 1984–5 harvest was about 85,000 tonnes, and cotton exports for 1984 were worth US$133.8m. Sugar exports for 1986 totalled 90,000 tonnes, 16,000 tonnes less than in 1985.

Beef exports fell from 37,000 tonnes in 1979 to 3000 tonnes in 1986, partially due to the clandestine slaughter and sale of animals on the black market and the smuggling of cattle over the Honduran and Costa Rican borders, as well as to increased domestic consumption. In 1984 Nicaragua asked to be removed from the list of countries eligible to export meat to the United States, hitherto its largest market, because it could no longer meet stringent laboratory testing requirements.

TABLE 8.2   AGRICULTURAL PRODUCTION 1983–1985

('000 tons)	1983	1984	1985
Maize	218	187	234
Rice	171	162	156
Sorghum	95	116	194
Beans	57	44	57
Sugar	2911	2545	2831
Bananas	128	128	127
Coffee	45	50	50
Cotton	80	85	69
Meat	62	59	59

Source: FAO

VI   Industry

The manufacturing sector accounts for about 25% of GDP and employs 18% of the workforce, although the sector has shrunk recently due to a shortage of foreign exchange, raw materials, imported machinery and skilled manpower, as well as lack of investment by the private sector, and grew by only 0.2% in 1984. The main employers—the textile, clothing, shoe and wood furniture industries—have all reduced their staffing levels. Most industry is state controlled and geared towards meeting domestic consumption and defence requirements. Apart from those listed, other industries include food processing, sugar refining, beverages and cooking oils, meat processing, and agro-allied industries based on textiles, tobacco, coffee, cocoa, rubber and timber.

The construction sector grew by 8% in 1985, similar to 1984 but less than in 1983 (16.7%). The sector was mainly concerned with strategic and low-cost housing projects and improving road networks connecting agricultural areas to market outlets. Work was in progress on an airfield at Punta Huete and a deep-water port at El Bluff on the east coast.

Mining, mainly of gold and silver, accounts for only a very small percentage of GDP and employs only a small number of workers. Most of the mines are in the north east in areas of contra activity, and production has been severely affected. However, a recovery began in 1986 as the contras were driven out of the area and Sweden, Czechoslovakia and Bulgaria increased their investment in the sector.

VII Energy

Wood accounts for over 50% of total energy consumption. All oil requirements are imported from the Comecon countries and Cuba, with small amounts from Libya, Algeria and Iran, and imports of oil and oil products in 1986 amounted to 5.46 million barrels. Oil was previously supplied by Venezuela and Mexico under the San José agreement concluded in 1980, but both these countries later suspended their side of the agreement because of Nicaragua's failure to pay for the oil. Geothermal power is being rapidly expanded, and already contributes about 20% of the country's total electricity requirements.

VIII External trade position

Nicaragua has had a trade deficit since 1980 which has steadily worsened from US$436.8m in 1980 to an estimated US$661.4m in 1986. Imports remained at about the same level in the first half of the 1980s, while exports declined, mainly due to falling world prices for cotton and sugar plus a drop in production for these two crops. Since the imposition in May 1985 of the trade embargo by the United States—until 1984 Nicaragua's largest single trading partner—and with the Central American Common Market ailing, Nicaragua has acquired new export markets in Western Europe (48% of total value in 1985 compared with 32% in 1980) and Japan (20%, compared with 3% in 1980), and imports from Comecon countries increased to 38.6% in 1985, compared to less than 1% in 1980.

TABLE 8.3 SECTORAL CONTRIBUTION TO GDP 1980–1985

(US$ mn)	1980	1984	1985
Agriculture	612	678	680
Mining	20	14	11
Manufacturing industry	676	740	701
Construction	77	80	87
Electricity, gas and water	56	51	53
Transport and communications	152	157	138
Commerce	590	493	470

Source: IADB

TABLE 8.4   FOREIGN TRADE 1980–1985

(US$ mn)	1980	1981	1982	1983	1984	1985
Exports	450	508	408	431	385	294
Imports	887	999	775	807	826	836
Balance	−437	−491	−367	−376	−441	−542

Source: CEPAL/Ministry of Foreign Trade/Instituto Nacional de Estadísticas y Censos

The trade embargo had the most immediate effect on the banana market. Sugar exports had already been curtailed by the United States the previous year. The continuing weak trade position contributed to a large current account deficit and to the accumulation of a huge external debt, estimated at more than US$5bn in 1986. Being unable to meet its debt obligations, Nicaragua has entered into a state of passive default whereby it repays only those creditors who agree to make further loans. Even so, its debt servicing obligations doubled in 1986. The approval by the IADB of a loan of US$58.4m for agricultural projects has been effectively blocked by the United States since 1982, despite Nicaragua's repayment in March 1986 of US$7.5m in arrears to the Bank. The main sources of credit are the Comecon countries (over 60% in 1984), Latin America (25%) and Western Europe (9%). Individual countries supplying aid and credits have included China, Peru, Sweden, Norway, Finland and Spain.

CHAPTER NINE
PANAMA

I Political structure

Panamanian politics continue to be dominated by the National Guard, despite a nominal return to democracy when Nicolás Ardito Barletta was elected President in May 1984. Even the election that brought him to power was widely viewed as fraudulent, with Ardito Barletta scraping home by a mere 1712 votes after the military had stopped the count and one person had been killed in subsequent protests. Although Barletta, a right-wing former World Bank economist standing for the Revolutionary Democratic Party (PRD), was the military's preferred candidate, he did not survive the displeasure of the National Guard chief, General Manuel Antonio Noriega Morena. After several warnings from the populist commander-in-chief about the social cost of austerity measures being pressed by the International Monetary Fund (IMF) and the World Bank, Barletta was replaced by his deputy, Eric Arturo Delvalle, in September 1985.

Barletta's training and experience left him without the political skills necessary to steer the country through the political and economic difficulties encountered during the adjustment process, and his successor has enjoyed much more success. However, Barletta's authority was fatally undermined by the way in which he came to power. Popular perceptions of fraud and military interference stripped his administration of credibility from the start. With no electoral power base, the President was even more dependent on the military than previous civilian heads of state whom the National Guard has appointed. The extent of military control of the political scene is personified by Barletta's opponent in the 1984 polls, Arnulfo Arias Madrid, leader of the Christian Democrat Party (PCD). The 1984 result, if indeed a fraud, represented the fourth time Arias had been denied presidential power by the military. In October 1968, Arias was overthrown for the third time by the military, whose power he had sought to curb. On this occasion, he had been in the National Palace for only 11 days.

The coup was to bring to power Colonel Omar Torrijos Herrera, who dominated Panamanian politics until his death in an air crash in 1981. Torrijos' brand of populist nationalism still dominates the political scene, and his memory is frequently invoked, particularly against the United States. This is largely a by-product of the successful outcome to Canal Treaty negotiations which dragged on throughout the 1970s. After a referendum in 1977, two separate treaties were ratified in 1979 and Panama will assume control of the Canal on 1 January in the year 2000.

Relations with Washington have been generally difficult since the death of Torrijos. The unceremonious ousting of Barletta, the upturn in Panamanian nationalism that has bent itself against the United States, and continued allegations concerning the laundering of cocaine-smuggling profits through the country's offshore banking system have all taken their toll on bilateral relations. Things came to a head in 1986 when the US State Department leaked allegations that Noriega was himself heavily involved in drug-smuggling and gun-running rackets. It was also claimed that he had passed US intelligence information to the Cuban leader, Fidel Castro. The allegations were front-page news in leading US newspapers. Noriega, however, survived, and his reputation as a strong man capable of standing up to the United States may even have been strengthened. Ironically, it has been the high-level US military presence in Panama in the past that has helped to boost the National Guard to their current position of power. The joint defence of the Canal agreed in 1979, and the withdrawal of the US Army's School of the Americas in 1984 mean that the number of American troops in the country has been radically cut. While this has led to a corresponding decline in US military influence in the country, the same is not true of the local National Guard, whose high-profile image on the political scene is a continuing obstacle to Washington's efforts to democratize the region.

II Demography

The population of Panama was estimated at 2.31 million in 1987, and the average annual growth rate is about 2.4%. Linking the Central-American isthmus and the South-American mainland, the country covers an area of 77,082 square kilometres. This gave a population density of 27.7 persons per square kilometre in 1984. In 1983, the country registered 26.2 live births and 4.1 deaths per 1000 inhabitants.

More than 85% of the population is of mixed blood, but there are significant concentrations of indigenous peoples in the remoter south-eastern province of Darien and south west of Panama City. More than 60% of the population is concentrated in urban areas, with Panama City accounting for nearly 40% of the total with about 910,000 inhabitants. The only other major towns are Colón, at the head of the Atlantic entrance to the Canal, and David, near the Costa Rican border. The two cities had populations estimated in 1985 at 172,000 and 83,000 respectively

The urban drift that is current throughout Central America has been accentuated in Panama by unemployment estimated at up to 20%, the relative strength of the manufacturing and re-export sectors and the inadequacy of agrarian reform policies. However, in other respects Panamanian demography is not typical of that in Latin America as a whole. The average size of a household is only 4.2 persons, according to the latest census (1980)—one of the lowest on the continent. Furthermore, the average age of the population has risen in recent years, rather than fallen, as in most Latin-American countries.

III Domestic economy

The Panamanian economy is founded on the services sector, with banking, commerce, the Canal, ship registration, distribution and various social services accounting for more than 70% of GDP in 1985. Dependence on services meant that the country was a little less vulnerable to the slump in commodity prices that hit other Central-American states in the early 1980s. However, the fall-off in world trade hit banking and revenue from Canal traffic and ship registration in Panama, and it was only major construction projects such as the completion of an oil pipeline across the country that saved the economy from deep recession in the early 1980s.

The economy recorded substantial growth until 1983, when there was an expansion of only 0.4%, followed by a similar level of shrinkage the following year. By 1985, growth was back to the levels of 1981, while expansion in 1986 was estimated at about 3%. However, per capita growth has fallen or remained stagnant in each year since 1982.

The basis of current government policy is the economic adjustment programme agreed with the World Bank and IMF in 1986. The basic aims are to diversify the economic base and boost exports and investment, while preserving jobs and the current level of social spending. The overall scheme includes reforms to the labour code, new industrial incentives and an agricultural development law. The strategy was a compromise between the demands of the multilateral aid agencies, which refused to back government debt rescheduling efforts with fresh credits unless major structural adjustments were pushed through, and the country's powerful labour sector, led by the Council of Organized Workers (Conato). The unions opposed the reforms to the labour code which threatened to reduce wages, and the privatization plans, which they feared would lead to redundancies.

The new industrial legislation progressively reduces import barriers over the next five years. New industry locating in Panama is eligible for tariff reductions of up to 60% in the first seven years and 40% subsequently. Export firms are now exempted from a variety of taxes, with special incentives for non-traditional foreign exchange earners and firms introducing new technology. The agricultural development law reduced farm subsidies, while the banking sector was liberalized to offer a wider range of modern services based on big telecommunications investments. A bond market is to be set up along with an insurance and reinsurance system.

The level of unemployment is hotly disputed. Conato puts national joblessness at more than 20%. The government claims the figure was 10.2% in 1986, when officials recorded a fall from 11.8%. The UN's Economic Commission on Latin America (ECLA) gave a figure of 9% in 1986, while independent sources in Panama say that unemployment is about 15%. Whatever the real figure, unemployment rose in the early 1980s because the new service sector industries were much less labour-intensive, while budget cuts forced on the government by debt servicing obligations saw no real growth in employment in the public sector. However, falling inflation since 1982 has seen the spending power of many people in work rise appreciably.

As the country uses the US dollar as its national currency, albeit renamed the balboa, inflation is intricately linked to that of Panama's main trading partners, particularly the United States. Big surges in money supply are unknown because the government cannot print its own notes. In 1986, inflation fell to an estimated 0.4%, a continuation of a trend that has seen prices fall steadily since a rise of 13.8% in the Consumer Price Index in 1980.

TABLE 9.1   BUDGET 1986–1987

(millions of balboas (= US$))	1986	% of total	1987	% of total
Income				
Current income	1010.3	61.3	1062.6	56.9
Capital income	612.2	37.1	780.1	41.8
of which – credit	578.5	–	758.3	–
– other capital	33.7	1.6	21.8	1.3
Other income	1649.4	100.0	1866.4	100.0
Expenditure				
Executive	755.0	45.8	847.4	45.4
of which – education	248.2	15.0	269.9	14.5
– health	90.2	5.5	123.6	6.6
Legislative	28.1	1.7	34.5	1.8
Judiciary	18.7	1.1	22.4	1.2
Electoral Board	6.3	0.4	6.5	0.4
Public debt	841.3	51.0	955.5	51.2

Panama has always registered budget deficits, and the shortfall between government spending and income has risen steadily since 1980, when the fiscal deficit was only 5% of GDP. The 1987 budget of US$1.87bn represented a 13% increase on the previous year, with government expenses not covered by income amounting to US$803.8m, equivalent to about 15% of GDP. Debt servicing as a proportion of total spending has more than doubled in the last eight years, rising from 23.6% in 1979 to a projected 51.2% in 1987.

IV   External position

With most of the country's foreign currency earnings coming from invisibles such as transportation and distribution services, banking, ship registration and tourism, Panama has always run a big deficit on merchandise trade. Agriculture and fishing account for more than 60% of visible exports, which reached a value of US$336.2m in 1985. Shipments of bananas earned a total of US$78.1m that year, a figure that has remained relatively stable since 1982. Shrimps were the second most valuable individual export, earning US$60.5m, up more than 20% on the previous year. The outlook for the country's next most important agricultural exports—coffee and sugar—is poor, despite the fact that coffee earnings virtually doubled in 1986, jumping from US$15.6m to US$29m. Sugar earnings will be hit by yet another round of cuts in the US sugar quota, an agreement by which

Washington pays a preferential price of about 22 cents per pound, nearly four times the 1985–6 international price. Sugar export earnings have dropped steadily from US$41.3m in 1983 to US$27.3m in 1985.

TABLE 9.2   FOREIGN TRADE (MERCHANDISE) 1983–1985

(fob in US$ mn)	1983	1984	1985
Exports			
Bananas	75.0	74.6	78.1
Shrimps	51.4	49.2	60.5
Sugar	41.3	33.0	27.3
Refined petroleum	35.8	5.3	20.0
Coffee	15.9	13.0	15.6
Clothing	7.6	9.3	11.5
Imports			
Manufactured goods	323.6	350.7	348.6
Capital goods	280.8	264.4	266.7
Oil and fuels	324.2	282.6	238.2
Chemicals	148.1	160.1	158.0
Foodstuffs	107.1	104.4	108.7

Source: Contraloría General (Panama)

Total merchandise imports were estimated at US$1.24bn in 1985, down from US$1.27bn the previous year. In 1985, manufactured goods were the biggest class of imports, reaching a value of US$348.6m, or 28.1% of the total. Capital goods imports, mostly industrial machinery and transport equipment, were worth US$266.7m or 21.5% of the total. However, the most notable feature of the country's import bill has been the fall in oil purchases as hydroelectricity has accounted for a steady increase in power generation. In 1985, crude oil cost a total of US$238.2m, or 19.2% of the total import bill, down from US$324.2m, or more than 25%, as recently as 1983.

One of the most salient features of Panama's foreign trade is the Colón Free Zone (CFZ), the second largest free-trade zone in the world. On the Caribbean side of the Canal, the CFZ has exploited its position at the head of the world's most vital shipping lane to build up a trade worth about US$3.4bn in 1985. More than 500 international manufacturing companies are located in the 50-hectare park, with more than 80% of Panama's exports and 50% of the country's imports originating through the zone. This gives the country's external account a high value of re-exports, about 60% of which go to

Latin-American states. Although CFZ trade has been badly hit by the reduced import capacity of Latin-American states, there are plans to double the size of the zone in an effort to recover the US$4.3bn volume of trade recorded in 1981. A diverse, integrated project called Centrepoint aims to improve links between the towns of Cristóbal and Balboa on the two coasts, and a computerized container port has already been opened on the Atlantic side. Certainly, there is no doubting the importance of the CFZ to the Panamanian economy. In 1985, its contribution to GDP was estimated at just under 3%.

In 1985, trade between Panama and the Central American Common Market (CACM) bucked the common trend and rose nearly US$3m to US$56.5m. Exports to El Salvador almost doubled, despite sharp drops in sales to Nicaragua and Honduras. Costa Rica remains the country's largest regional trading partner, selling US$25.4m worth of goods and buying US$16m worth. In 1985, the United States accounted for about 60% of merchandise exports and provided about one-third of total imports.

Panama has one of the highest per capita debts in Latin America, and the debt-service burden has soared as a result of the terms on the loans and higher interest rates. In 1983, the government agreed to meet IMF conditions for an 18-month standby loan of US$155m, and a rescheduling of some US$180m owed to commercial creditors took place in September of that year. A much bigger rescheduling took place two years later, when US$603m falling due in 1985–6 was restructured. This package included the renewal of US$220m worth of short-term credit lines and fresh credits worth a total of US$60m. Neither of these has proved sufficient to allay the worst effects of the bunching of payments. Total external liabilities were put at US$5.1bn in 1986, and more than US$1bn in payments due before the end of the decade will have to be rescheduled. The proportion of total spending used on debt servicing is expected to continue to rise until such a major restructuring comes into effect. By 1987, debt servicing, including interest and amortization payments, was over 50% of total government spending, having doubled as a proportion of the budget in less than a decade.

V Structure of production

Transport and communications is the largest single sector of GDP as a result of the Canal and ship registration. Passage fees rose slightly in 1985 to US$301m after declining in both 1983 and 1984 from the US$326m level of 1982. The main reason was a fall in traffic as a result of both the decline in world trade and the completion of the trans-Panamanian pipeline that now transports much of the crude oil that formerly passed through the Canal. Ship registration fees have tripled in less than a decade, reaching US$36.4m last year as the country had boosted its share of world ship registries from 12.2% to 16.3% between 1983 and 1986. Income from related shipping business such as taxes, mortgages and corporate services brought in another US$42m in 1986. While Panama is now second only to Liberia in terms of international ship registration, reduced fees and lower taxes announced in 1987 are expected to boost the country's position further by the end of the decade.

TABLE 9.3   STRUCTURE OF GDP 1980 AND 1985

(in US$ mn at 1970 prices)	1980	% of total	1985	% of total
Agriculture	173.7	9.9	196.9	9.9
Manufacturing	182.1	10.4	177.4	8.9
Distribution services	256.4	14.7	243.2	12.3
Financial services	227.2	13.0	276.3	13.9
Transport and communications	207.6	11.9	323.8	16.3
Mining	3.1	0.2	2.5	0.1
Construction	124.3	7.1	93.4	4.7
Electricity, gas and water	53.5	3.1	68.1	3.4
Canal commission	175.5	10.1	177.0	8.9

Source: Contraloría General (Panama)

Financial services are the second most important sector of GDP, contributing 13.9% of the total in 1985. Panama is a major offshore banking haven, with total deposits rising US$2bn in 1985 to reach US$28.3bn. The increase reversed the fall witnessed since total deposits reach an all-time high of US$36.8bn in 1982. The rise was largely attributable to deposits from Latin-American nations involved in disputes with creditors over debt repayments. Peru, Brazil and Nicaragua were all known to have withdrawn funds from US banks in case of seizure during 1985–6. The main attraction of Panama as an offshore banking haven remains its use of the US dollar as national currency. This asset has been complemented by liberal banking regulations and the abolition of currency controls. There are about 120 international banks operating in the country, a number that includes all the largest groups, and the government has tried to give the sector a further boost by more deregulation in 1986.

However, the liberal nature of the country's banking laws and the government's traditional nationalism in opposing US demands have brought Panama City into sharp conflict with Washington over the supply of bank-account information in suspected drugs-smuggling cases. Like most Caribbean Basin offshore banking havens, Panama maintains that any compromise of its secrecy laws would damage business. The US Government, for its part, holds that Panama is now the drug smugglers' favourite location for laundering illegal earnings.

Agricultural contribution to total GDP was 9.9% in 1985, but the sector employs more than a quarter of the national workforce, and traditional crops account for more than 60% of merchandise exports. The main crops remain bananas and sugar, although production of the latter is increasingly confined to the domestic market. The Chiriquí Land Company, a subsidiary of United Brands, accounts for three-quarters of national banana production. Rice, sorghum, maize and beans are the main staple crops, with significant quantities of the last two having to be imported.

TABLE 9.4   AGRICULTURAL PRODUCTION 1981–1985

('000 tons)	1981	1982	1983	1984	1985^e
Sugar	2590	2094	2134	2096	1980
Bananas	1045	1057	1100	1062	1128
Rice	198	178	202	177	202
Maize	58	67	75	72	75
Beans	3	2	3	3	2
Coffee	7	8	9	9	11

Source: FAO (1981–84)/Contraloría General (Panama, 1985)
Note: ^{e} – estimate

Both the livestock and fishing sectors have increased in importance during the last ten years. The country is one of the world's largest exporters of shrimps, which earned a total of US$60.5m in 1985. Fresh and processed fish, plus lobster, are also significant exports. Livestock production showed consistent growth of nearly 5% per annum in the five years to 1985, when the national herd stood at 1.52 million head of cattle. Slaughter levels grew 20% in the five years to 1986, to top the 300,000 mark.

Manufacturing accounted for 8.9% of total GDP in 1985, but the sector is heavily dependent on the Colón Free Zone (CFZ), which has tended to hold back domestic development rather than stimulate it. Most of the more than 500 companies in the CFZ are simply re-export or assembly operations, while the availability of consumer goods through the Canal Zone has tended to discourage local development. Food and fish processing is the main activity, with most of the diversification into steel, cement and textile plants that has taken place coming as a result of government investment.

Three major hydroelectric plants, the largest being the 300 MW La Fortuna near David, have reduced the need for imported crude oil to generate electricity. Hydroelectricity now accounts for about 10% of total output, but with no known oil reserves, Panama will remain a significant importer of crude. Despite deposits of gold, silver, copper and coal, there is little mining activity. Copper is abundant, but development of the most important deposit at Cerro Colorado in Chiriquí has been postponed by the multinational Rio Tinto Zinc because of low world prices. However, exploration programmes undertaken by the US mineral firm Freeport could lead to the opening up of the eastern jungle province of Darien, where there are known deposits of gold and porphyry copper.

VI   Consumption, standard of living

The lowest level of inflation in Latin America, the large inflow of consumer goods through the Canal and Colón Free Zones and a high level of liquidity all stimulated consumption throughout the 1970s in Panama. The most powerful trade union movement in the region has kept nominal wage rise settlements well ahead of inflation since 1982. However, these trends were counteracted by economic stagnation in 1983 and 1984 and per capita declines of 2.0% and 2.3% in economic growth in the same years.

The budgetary constraints imposed by the spiralling level of debt payments have caused government consumption to fall steadily since 1982. In 1985, state consumption slumped 5.9% to US$297.6m at 1970 prices. Private consumption has increased, but at a much slower rate than in the 1970s. In 1985, private demand rose a marginal 2.6%. The chronic debt problem leaves little scope for immediate improvement in the state sector, while private consumption will depend largely on the amount by which wage settlements exceed inflation and world trade trends. Panama's key manufacturing,

135

banking and transport sectors remain critically dependent on the strength of international commerce. Nearly two-thirds of the ships using the Canal carry US and Japanese goods, while more than 60% of the country's re-exports are destined for Latin-American countries.

TABLE 9.5   CONSUMPTION INDICATORS 1981–1985

	1981	1982	1983	1984	1985
GDP growth (%)	4.2	5.5	0.4	−0.4	4.1
GDP growth per capita (%)	2.0	0.3	−2.0	−2.3	1.7
Private consumption (in US$ mn at 1970 prices)	945.7	997.6	1053.5	1194.3	1225.0
Government consumption (in US$ mn at 1970 prices)	334.9	365.5	343.8	316.3	297.6
Consumer prices (% growth)	7.3	4.3	2.1	1.6	1.0
Nominal salaries (% growth)	4.2	6.1	3.8	3.6	4.2

Source: Controlaría General (Panama)/International Monetary Fund

The success of the service industry sector throughout the 1970s has combined with the populist policies of successive governments to give the country a relatively high standard of living by Latin-American standards. Life expectancy is high, at 71 years for males and 73 years for females, while the infant mortality rate is exceptionally low at 21 per 1000 live births. There is one doctor for every 1080 Panamanians, and literacy and school enrolment are high, both standing at 87%. Despite budgetary pressures, spending on social services has been maintained. Expenditure on health and education was increased 35% and 8% respectively in the 1987 budget.

Consumption indicators are also very high by Latin-American standards. There are more than 60 cars in use per 1000 population, and one in eight Panamanians owns a television set. However, all these figures are artificially inflated by consumption in the Canal Zone. In reality, consumption in Panama is even more concentrated than in the country's neighbours, being confined to Panama City, Colón and the Canal area. In the countryside the standard of living remains low, with the population that is confined to rural areas, as for that in the urban slums, excluded from the benefits of the country's rather unique economy.

CHAPTER TEN
FUTURE OUTLOOK

I Key issues and prospects

The key issues affecting the future of the Mexican and Central-American economies can be classified into four categories: international trade, the regional economy, the domestic economies and debt. The chief political issue will remain the resolution of the Central-American conflicts: the internal ones in Guatemala and El Salvador, and that between the USA and Nicaragua.

All these countries are dependent, though in different ways, on the recovery in world trade and an increase in commodity prices. Oil prices are crucial to the functioning of the Mexican economy, bananas and coffee to the others, and Panama, with its Canal and free-trade zone, benefits from increased prices and expanding trade. More specifically, all the countries with their close links to the USA (except, for the time being, Nicaragua) would be damaged by a US recession and boosted by US expansion. Recession or expansion in the USA would affect the demand for their primary products and manufactured goods, levels of aid and investment, and the levels of migration from them to the USA. The smaller countries are more vulnerable than Mexico, but all are exposed to the winds from the north.

The experience of the Central American Common Market members in the recession of the 1980s might convince them that the problems of having a common market are less than those caused by not having one. Plainly, the problems that caused the original breakdown have not disappeared: the 1980s have not removed the unevenness of development in the region, nor have they diminished the balance of payments problems that induced protectionism among the members of the CACM. Protectionist sentiment and actions are not confined to Central America, and the actions of the USA, Europe and Latin-American countries to a lesser extent could prove much more problematic than the internal disputes which wrecked the CACM in the 1970s. The increasing involvement of Panama, as its relationship with the USA continues to change and develop, and Mexican assistance during the oil crisis perhaps developing into a greater involvement with Central America (and there are signs of this already), may lead in time to a larger and better regional grouping. With the experience of the CACM it may then be possible to avoid some of the mistakes of the past.

The major issues affecting the domestic economies are industrialization and the interrelated issues of land reform and the redistribution of resources.

Industrialization, as in many other developing countries, is both essential and problematic. Mexico, with its large population, natural resources and energy supplies, clearly has problems of a different order to those of the other states. Mexican industrialization, like that of other large Latin-American countries, was based on import substitution. Like the others, it has run into two main problems. First, many of these industries were relatively inefficient, and their protection from foreign competition exacerbated that problem. Second, population growth ate into growth rates with the result that the internal market may have grown in numbers but not enough in purchasing power. The other countries, with their much smaller markets and poorer populations, had to look mainly to exports for their industrial effort. The Central American Common Market was an attempt to increase the size of this market, but its protection meant that Guatemala and El Salvador benefited the most and became even more clearly export oriented with the break-up of the CACM. At the moment, therefore, strong recoveries in these countries await the general overall recovery. The free-zone sectors of Mexico and Panama are cushioned against the recession by their status. In the case of Panama, industrialization is not as important as in the other countries.

The issues of land reform and the redistribution of resources can be taken together. The case for land reform in the region remains much the same in the 1980s as it was in Mexico more than half a century ago. The largest land holdings may be efficiently run, but the cultivated areas are often small fractions of the whole. The rest of the land is held to keep it out of the hands of the rural poor so that large supplies of cheap labour remain available. This has been the policy of both local elites and foreign companies. This large pool of landless or practically landless labourers has been one of the major sources of political instability in the region. By keeping large numbers of people in poverty, it also affects adversely attempts to industrialize, since domestic demand is quite weak for manufacturers. Government expenditure tends, because of this situation, to be biased towards its policing functions and away from welfare services. Populations remain poorly fed and educated, and in poor health. They therefore constitute populations hardly ideal for countries contemplating the demands of modern industrial society, although better than many African and Asian populations.

The bias towards policing rather than welfare also allows local elites to maintain fairly low levels of taxation. Indeed, some critics point to the ways in which local elites have avoided these issues: (1) by using foreign borrowing as a substitute for higher taxation, (2) by using foreign savings as a substitute for tapping internal savings, and (3) by postponing land reform by colonization schemes on state lands. Thus, the potential benefits of the long boom from the 1950s to the 1970s became actual benefits for the elite and the expanding middle classes, but left untouched the vast majority of people in the region.

The prospects for major changes on these issues look dim. In the immediate future, a mixture of US economic and military aid will assist the elites in postponing hard decisions of benefit to the majority but with immediate, less beneficial effects on themselves.

Debt remains the last, but not least, of these major problems. Again, a distinction can be made between Mexico and the rest. Mexico, like many other oil producers but especially those with large populations, borrowed not simply as a replacement for domestic savings but to enable it to accelerate development by engaging in an even wider range of activities than would otherwise have been possible. Much of the borrowing, which with hindsight appears unwise, in the heady days of the 1973 and 1979 oil price rises, when many believed prices would hold those levels, appeared all too wise. The saving grace for Mexico, if not for the bankers who all too willingly lent, is the size of the debt, which offers leverage on creditors. The Central-American countries borrowed to avoid redistribution through taxation, and being much smaller debtors have little leverage. The leverage they have is political: the knowledge that the USA will bail them out so long as it retains its strategic interest in the region. Since there can be little prospect of that interest disappearing in the foreseeable future, their debt problems are hardly as severe as those of many other countries with rather better reasons for being in debt.

The political issue will remain of fundamental importance. The USA/Nicaragua conflict touches other Central-American countries: Costa Rica and Honduras have been affected by the presence of

US-backed contra forces. The resolution of the conflict is unlikely to solve the problem of heavily armed men in the region who are not part of regular armies and who have no wars to fight. Such a state would be an improvement on the present situation, but seems very distant at the moment. Without political solutions to present problems, the massive diversion of resources into the sterile and deadly military sector will continue, hindering attempts in Nicaragua, El Salvador and Guatemala to develop the economies and fight poverty.

II   Economic forecasts by country

Nicaragua

Of the region's countries, Nicaragua would benefit most from an end to hostilities. The destruction of the capital, Managua, in 1972 had not been made good when further disruption to the economy occurred during the civil war of 1978–9. In the 1980s the mining of harbours, attacks on oil installations, and the destruction of agricultural enterprises and infrastructure have all been the consequences of the US-backed anti-government forces. Resources which could have been devoted to repairing damage inflicted in 1979 and before have had to be diverted to defence. The US trade embargo begun in 1985, although aid had already been cut off in 1981, has had a damaging impact (since pre-1981 trade links had been so close) despite Nicaraguan attempts to diversify their trading partners. Cuba in the 1960s went through a similar difficult period of adjustment.

If the conflict continues, the problems of the Nicaraguan economy will continue to mulitply. Internally it will run into even greater problems with its private sector, and continued land reform will not be able to satisfy urban workers in times of growing austerity. The longer the revolution survives, the longer away will be the bad old days, and present conditions rather than the memory of even worse conditions in the past will shape people's actions. Attacks on the economy will seriously affect Nicaragua's ability to export and to earn foreign exchange and service its debt. The Soviet Union and Eastern Bloc will not wish to shoulder a burden even greater than Cuba in the western hemisphere when the economic and political returns are so limited.

If any of the peace plans work, the future would be somewhat brighter. The diversion of resources to the military would be halted, attacks on the economy would end, and presumably normal relations with the USA would be re-established. Industry would then benefit from foreign and domestic investment. Part of the August 1987 peace plan is a programme of aid to Nicaragua, which since 1985 has not been part of the San José agreements with Mexico and Venezuela on oil supplies because it was unable to keep up its payments. Ensured oil supplies and expanding industry would revitalize the economy, along with increased agricultural production for export, rather than the current necessity to concentrate food production on domestic consumption.

In either case, Nicaragua will have enormous problems of economic reconstruction at a time when its principal exports, coffee and cotton, despite the odd boom (as that for coffee in 1986), fetch prices that tend to fluctuate at low levels, while its debt servicing remains very high, and its industrial exports suffer from the continuing recession of world trade.

El Salvador

As for Nicaragua, the end of political violence would also boost the El Salvador economy. With over a quarter of the government budget devoted to defence, there is much scope for re-directing expenditure to more economically useful ends. Here, however, an end to the conflict may have paradoxical effects. At the moment, El Salvador benefits from sizeable US aid; the end of conflict may reduce this flow. This, at least, was the experience of Grenada after democratic government had been restored in 1984. The end of the conflict would also have to mean concessions to the anti-government forces, especially in land reform and trade union rights, as well as more democratic procedures. These reforms would imply great changes in the existing economic order which might threaten the viability of enterprises dependent on low-paid labour in industry and agriculture, since costs would rise and existing advantages disappear. Such changes would be resisted by influential sectors of the private sector, with disruptive effects on the economy. Whatever the difficulties of peace, they would appear to be much less than the continuation of war.

If the conflict does continue, levels of US aid are likely to remain high without doing much to solve the country's problems. High population densities and limited land reform will also continue to fuel emigration. Industry will continue to expand, but the general level of development in the region, low purchasing power domestically, labour problems and guerrilla attacks will slow the pace of development. The agriculture sector will continue to suffer especially, since guerrillas operate in agricultural areas. As in the past, exports will be adversely affected, widening the trade deficit and increasing foreign exchange and debt servicing problems.

As with Nicaragua, major problems will persist whether the internal conflict ends or not: debts, poor prices, the necessity for further industrialization, and high unemployment.

Guatemala

Some improvements in the political sphere mean that Guatemala has a slightly better future than Nicaragua and El Salvador, a condition that seemed unlikely during the period of intense guerrilla activity and death squads in the late 1970s and early 1980s. As in these countries, however, the basic problems are lack of diversification, low purchasing power, low taxation (which the Nicaraguans have tackled), and excessive expenditure on the military. Like them, too, poor prices for exports remain a major problem. The relatively strong and diversified industrial sector should make an increasingly important contribution to the economy, but industrial relations will prove a crucial issue. If wages are kept low, worker militancy will flare again; low wages also mean that purchasing power remains low, stifling domestic demand for both agricultural and industrial products. The level of industrial development does mean that the prospects for dealing with the problems of unemployment are brighter than elsewhere, but the size of the agricultural sector labour force does suggest that such optimism is only relative. Potentially, the petroleum industry may compensate for the deficiences of agriculture and industry. Difficulties of quality and access and lower oil prices mean that such a contribution depends on increased demand and higher prices making Guatemalan oil profitable to extract. Similar prospects affect copper mining, with current low prices affecting output. A strong recovery in world industrial production and trade would benefit the Guatemalan mining sector. As in other countries, short-term prospects are very much affected by the austerity programmes which reduce consumption. In the long term, the development of the country depends on better communications, the lack of which affects oil production and leaves areas in the north and west with little connection with the rest of the country.

Honduras

Honduras, with its greater political stability than El Salvador and Guatemala and lesser population density relieving the pressure for land reform, faces a less troubled future than those countries. The main threat to its stability comes from the violence elsewhere in the region and the massive American military presence. There seems little short-term prospect for Honduras becoming less dependent on bananas and coffee for its main exports. Since prices for these are not likely to be very buoyant, the economy is likely to remain fairly stagnant. Austerity measures, which will persist, will continue to depress domestic demand. The low level of industrialization, and its comparatively underdeveloped nature, does not suggest that very much can be expected from that sector. Much can be expected, however, from infrastructural improvements (Honduras possesses the only capital in the region with no railway connection) in stimulating development, and current developments should bear fruit in the medium term. Much will depend, too, in the medium and long terms on greater investment to diversify the economy. Unemployment and underemployment will prove more serious problems while population growth continues at high levels and growth continues to be sluggish. Peace in the region may result in less US interest and thus reduced aid. This suggests that Honduras, of all the countries in the region, has acquired an interest in maintaining the status quo. Debt servicing will remain a significant problem in both the short and long terms. Current measures to improve export performance and take advantage of the Caribbean Basin Initiative are unlikely to prove of great significance in solving Honduras' economic problems.

Costa Rica

For a long time it looked as if Costa Rica would be engulfed in regional conflict. That danger seems to have passed, but ideological differences within the country have been strengthened. Combined with the strains caused by the current economic crisis, Costa Rican politics has entered a phase of instability not seen since the 1940s. Not having a large army with an untouchable budget, Costa Rica has been able, unlike other countries in the region, to implement a wide range of IMF adjustment measures. The country's large social security system is, however, sacrosanct, and will continue to prove a source of disagreement between those who feel that it can be cut and their opponents. Current policies (devaluation, tax concessions), together with the tariff concessions of the CBI, will continue to stimulate foreign investment in Costa Rica, though foreign companies will continue to face foreign exchange problems. Investment in industry, a good infrastructure and high-quality labour force will ensure the expansion of non-agricultural exports. Agriculture, however, will remain the mainstay of the economy in the foreseeable future. As for its neighbours, coffee, bananas and cattle will continue to be subject to fluctuating prices, though diversification into the export of flowers, fruit and vegetables will expand and help to compensate for falls in the prices of the main exports. Economic support from the USA will, even if the conflict ends, remain high; Costa Rica is nearer to the Panama Canal than those countries that currently excite Washington's interests. Long-term prospects for development are minerals, bauxite, iron ore, manganese and sulphur. Infrastructural improvements are also a long-term necessity, despite its superiority to other states. Continued growth and development, in the short and long terms, depend on the debt crisis being safely negotiated. Although this will be a very difficult task, the prospects are favourable.

Panama

Although its export sector resembles that of the other Central-American states (bananas, shrimps and sugar being the leading exports), its size is small. Like the others, Panama depends on the recovery of world trade for continuing growth, but unlike them, strong demand not for its agricultural products but for its services is the key. Its manufacturing sector also is comparatively small and not well integrated with the rest of the economy, since the Colón Free Zone engages in re-assembly or re-export activities. As in the other countries, unemployment and heavy debts are serious, and recent stirrings of middle-class political activity suggest that its period of relative political calm may be ending. In both the short and long terms, financial services, the Canal and ship registration will provide the major sources of foreign exchange. Its offshore banking will continue to benefit from the large amount of money avoiding the stricter regulations and scrutiny of the major financial centres. This is a logical progression from the flag-of-convenience service Panama offered to ship-owners, now of lesser importance because of shrinking merchant fleets and competitors offering the same services. Offshore banking will continue to be strong, since Panama has several advantages over many of its competitors: its established position, its proximity to both the USA and South America with drugs-related money seeking a haven, its strong position enabling it to resist US pressure for disclosure, and its location at an international crossroads. New measures on ship registration are expected in the short term to boost this sector, but its long-term significance will decline. The Canal has been affected by the trans-isthmian pipeline transporting oil which formerly used the Canal, but further improvements in the Canal will be needed in the future. The debt problem will remain important, especially since measures adopted at the insistence of the IMF and World Bank are regarded as detrimental by workers. On the base of its financial and transport services, Panama faces a future rather more favourable in the short and long terms than its neighbours.

Mexico

Mexico's problems and prospects are of a different order to those of the Central-American states. Its mineral wealth—oil, gas, silver and other metals—its developing industries, and its agricultural sector exhibit basic strength and in the long term should enable the Mexican economy to develop into a major force in the world economy. Its stable political system, its high levels of education and large population provide the bases of a strong economy. Population growth, especially the growth of urban populations, constitutes a long-term threat to that potential, despite recent government efforts to develop under-populated regions. Reducing population growth will be the single greatest problem affecting long-term growth. In the short and medium terms, debt remains the great issue. Major efforts on the part of Mexico, its creditors and international agencies will have to continue. Excessively restrictive fiscal measures will affect Mexican ability to repay the debts, and threaten political stability. The size of the Mexican debt does give it leverage that its smaller neighbours do not possess in dealing with their creditors; its important place in Latin America, with its other large debtors, reinforces its bargaining power. On the other hand, continuing dependence on emigration, temporary and permanent, to the USA, and the importance of the US-owned industries in the northern border areas do tie Mexican hands. Oil and manufacturing will remain the important sectors, along with agricultural exports to the USA. Mexico will begin to play an even greater role in Central-American political and economic affairs, although continuing low prices for oil will restrict that role to a much smaller one than seemed likely in the 1970s.

III Outlook

The problem of debt will be the major short- and medium-term problem for all these countries. Mexico and Panama have the best prospects over the short and long terms, since they possess quite diversified economies, with Mexican potential the greater. For the other countries, export diversification and industrialization are essential but will have limited effects, especially in El Salvador, Guatemala and Honduras where land and taxation reforms are needed to ensure redistribution. The Nicaraguan experiment will depend for its success on the cessation of hostilities and an avoidance of the many mistakes made during similar experiments elsewhere. Costa Rica will face the tricky problem of retaining its effective social welfare system in a time of austerity. These five nations, with their similar economies, will continue to suffer from the poverty of their populations and being competitive with, rather than complementary to, each other. The expansion of manufacturing and the diversification of export agriculture will continue, but will depend heavily on the expansion of the world economy. Even, however, with a strong international expansion, these economies will continue to provide low standards of living for the majority of their citizens. Major improvements are not likely in the period to the end of the century. The region will remain poor and unstable for some time.

TABLE 10.1   POPULATION FORECASTS 1985–2000

	Population (millions)		Average annual growth rates 1985–2000 (%)	
	1990	**2000**	**Population**	**Labour force**
Costa Rica	3	3	1.9	2.4
El Salvador	5	6	2.0	3.3
Guatemala	9	12	2.5	3.3
Honduras	5	7	3.0	3.9
Mexico	89	110	2.2	3.0
Nicaragua	4	5	2.9	3.9
Panama	2	3	1.6	2.6

Source: World Development Report 1987

TABLE 10.2   PRODUCTION FORECASTS 1985–1995

	Growth Rates 1985–1995 (%)	Exports	
		1990	**1995**
Coffee		'000s of 60 kg bags	
El Salvador	1.4	2800	3000
Guatemala	0.8	2300	2450
Bananas		'000 tons	
Costa Rica	1.8	1027	1126
Honduras	1.4	986	1077
Panama	0.4	550	560
Energy		Million tons of oil equivalent	
Mexico: production	2.8	207	285
Mexico: consumption	4.5	117	198

Source: World Bank Price Prospects for Primary Commodities Vol. II (1984), Vol. V (1986)

TABLE 10.3 CENTRAL-AMERICAN MAJOR EXPORTS: PRICE FORECASTS 1990–2000 (1985 dollars)

		1986 (actual)	1990	1995	2000
Petroleum	($/bbl)	11.4	13.9	17.3	24.7
Coffee	(¢/kg)	361	267	270	277
Sugar	($/MT)	112	213	243	255
Beef	(¢/kg)	176	205	255	276
Bananas	($/MT)	336	349	335	321

Source: World Bank/International Finance Corporation Feb. 1987
Half Year Review of Commodity Price Forecasts and Quarterly Return of
Commodity Markets for December 1986

FACTFILE

TABLE 11.1   GROSS DOMESTIC PRODUCT, CURRENT PRICES 1980–1986

	Unit	1980	1981	1982	1983	1984	1985	1986
Costa Rica	m Colon	41406	57103	97505	126337	163011	192245	236841
El Salvador	m Colon	8917	8647	8966	10152	11657	14331	19895
Guatemala	m Quetzal	7879	8608	8728	9035	9397	n.a.	n.a.
Honduras	m Lempira	4976	5293	5582	5901	6299	6724	7237
Mexico	bn Pesos	4277	5874	9417	17142	28749	45589	84406e
Nicaragua	m Cordoba	21892	25773	29696	35783	37730	39000e	41000e
Panama	m Balboa	3559	3878	4278	4374	4566	4882	5000e

Source; IMF/Euromonitor/national statistics
Note: e estimates

**TABLE 11.2   PER CAPITA GROSS DOMESTIC PRODUCT,
CURRENT AND 1986 US DOLLARS, 1980 AND 1985**

	1980		1985	
	Current dollars	Dec. 1986 dollars	Current dollars	Dec. 1986 dollars
Costa Rica	2147	312	1466	1255
El Salvador	791	791	1189	1189
Guatemala	1139	1139	1256	1256
Honduras	674	674	769	769
Mexico	2686	67	2268	636
Nicaragua	798	115	450	170
Panama	1873	1873	2239	2239

Source: IMF/Euromonitor

**TABLE 11.3   REAL DEVELOPMENT OF GROSS DOMESTIC PRODUCT
1980–1986**

(base: 1980 = 100)	1980	1981	1982	1983	1984	1985	1986
Costa Rica	100.0	97.7	90.4	93.3	100.3	101.9	105.2
El Salvador	100.0	91.7	86.6	87.3	89.2	91.0	92.0
Guatemala	100.0	100.7	97.1	94.5	n.a.	n.a.	n.a.
Honduras	100.0	101.2	99.4	99.1	101.6	104.6	107.7
Mexico	100.0	107.9	107.4	101.7	105.4	108.3	n.a.
Nicaragua	100.0	105.4	104.6	109.2	107.6	104.8	n.a.
Panama	100.0	104.2	109.9	110.3	109.8	114.4	n.a.

Source: Euromonitor/IMF

**TABLE 11.4 COMPOSITION OF GROSS DOMESTIC PRODUCT,
BY DEMAND STRUCTURE**
(Percentage of total GDP: latest available information)

	Year	Government consumption	Private consumption	Fixed capital formation	Exports	Imports	Stock-building
Costa Rica	1986	16.8	59.8	19.2	32.1	−31.2	4.4
El Salvador	1986	13.7	79.3	12.8	23.2	−29.5	0.4
Guatemala	1984	7.7	84.5	9.8	13.1	−15.4	0.3
Honduras	1986	15.8	70.8	14.5	28.6	−30.6	0.7
Mexico	1985	9.9	66.2	16.9	12.1	−7.8	2.6
Nicaragua	1983	27.3	66.0	15.0	12.6	−23.1	2.2
Panama	1985	21.3	63.3	15.1	35.7	−34.8	−0.5

Source: Euromonitor/IMF

**TABLE 11.5 STRUCTURE OF PRODUCTION,
BY MAIN SUPPLY CATEGORIES**
(Data for 1985/6; expressed as a percentage of GDP)

	Agriculture	Manufacturing	Mining[1]	Construction	Others
Costa Rica	19.6	22.0	1.0	4.6	52.8
El Salvador	20.8	15.8	0.2	3.4	59.8
Guatemala	25.5	15.6	0.2	1.8	56.9
Honduras	25.5	12.4	1.8	1.8	58.5
Mexico	8.8	24.4	9.5	5.0	52.3
Nicaragua	31.8	32.8	0.5	4.1	30.8
Panama	9.9	8.9	4.7	3.4	73.1

Source: IMF/national statistics/Euromonitor
Note: [1] including petroleum and natural gas

TABLE 11.6 STRUCTURE OF MANUFACTURING 1970–1984

	Food 1970	Food 1984	Textiles/clothing 1970	Textiles/clothing 1984	Machinery/transport 1970	Machinery/transport 1984	Chemicals 1970	Chemicals 1984	Others 1970	Others 1984
Costa Rica	55	n.a.	8	n.a.	6	n.a.	8	n.a.	23	n.a.
El Salvador	46	40	24	22	4	6	3	10	24	21
Guatemala	39	n.a.	16	n.a.	n.a.	17	n.a.	24	n.a.	n.a.
Honduras	43	48	13	11	0	1	2	5	41	35
Mexico	29	28	16	12	11	13	9	13	35	34
Nicaragua	60	62	10	14	2	1	11	7	17	16
Panama	30	42	10	11	1	1	4	8	55	37

Source: World Bank Development Report 1987

TABLE 11.7   AGRICULTURAL DEVELOPMENT AND FERTILIZER USE 1970–1985

| | Agricultural value added (millions of 1980 dollars) | | Fertilizer consumption (hundred gm of plant nutrient per hectare of arable land) | | Cereal imports ('000 tonnes) | | Food aid in cereals ('000 tonnes) | | Average index of per capita food production (1979–81 = 100) |
	1970	1985	1970	1980	1970	1984	1970	1984	1983–1985
Costa Rica	666	949	1086	1391	110	146	1	164	100
El Salvador	740	847	1048	1132	75	224	4	194	100
Guatemala	n.a.	n.a.	224	375	138	164	9	23	108
Honduras	477	702	160	159	52	99	31	118	104
Mexico	11125	17669	246	602	2881	4507	n.a.	6	110
Nicaragua	400	533	184	557	44	114	3	43	90
Panama	275	375	391	411	63	115	3	1	109

Source: World Bank Development Report 1987

TABLE 11.8   DEVELOPMENT OF AGRICULTURAL PRODUCTION 1980–1985

(base: 1980=100)	1980	1981	1982	1983	1984	1985
Costa Rica	100.0	102.1	98.1	99.3	98.4	98.1
El Salvador	100.0	90.6	86.7	90.6	94.4	95.0
Guatemala	100.1	96.1	92.6	91.6	90.5	88.0
Honduras	100.0	105.8	108.2	110.1	112.7	114.3
Mexico	100.0	105.4	99.2	106.1	103.6	107.5
Nicaragua	100.0	114.2	118.2	113.8	115.4	118.0
Panama	100.0	104.5	106.3	107.1	108.0	108.5

Source: Euromonitor estimates, based on national statistics

TABLE 11.9   DEVELOPMENT OF PETROLEUM PRODUCTION IN SELECTED COUNTRIES 1980–1985

(1980=100)	1980	1981	1982	1983	1984	1985
Guatemala	100.0	104.0	160.2	178.4	190.0e	200.0e
Mexico	100.0	113.1	139.1	136.2	141.5	140.9

Source: Euromonitor/IMF
Note: e estimates

151

TABLE 11.10   TOURIST ARRIVALS IN SELECTED COUNTRIES 1980–1985

('000s)	1980	1981	1982	1983	1984	1985
Costa Rica	360	333	372	326	310e	325e
Mexico	4150	4250	3768	4749	4654	4207
Panama	375	364	370	335	302	300

Source: National statistical agencies
Note: e estimates

TABLE 11.11   COMMERCIAL ENERGY PRODUCTION AND CONSUMPTION 1965–1985

| | Average annual growth rate (%) | | | | Energy consumption per capita (kg of oil equivalent) | | Energy imports as a percentage of merchandise exports | |
| | Energy production | | Energy consumption | | | | | |
	1965–80	1980–85	1965–80	1980–85	1965	1985	1965	1985
Costa Rica	8.2	7.1	8.8	0.6	269	534	8	14
El Salvador	9.0	3.1	7.0	0.9	140	186	5	n.a.
Guatemala	12.5	7.2	6.8	−2.7	150	176	9	17
Honduras	14.0	2.5	7.6	1.7	111	201	5	28
Mexico	9.7	4.8	7.9	1.2	622	1290	4	1
Nicaragua	2.6	1.0	6.5	0.3	172	259	6	21
Panama	6.9	11.1	5.9	0.5	576	634	n.a.	n.a.

Source: World Bank Development Report

TABLE 11.12   EXPORTS 1980–1986

(US$mn, fob)	1980	1981	1982	1983	1984	1985	1986e
Costa Rica	1001	1003	870	882	1006	962	1357
El Salvador	1074	798	699	735	726	709	1850
Guatemala	1520	1291	1170	1092	1132	1060	950
Honduras	850	783	677	699	746	835	1037
Mexico	16066	19938	21230	22312	24196	21867	16483
Nicaragua	450	508	406	431	385	294	250
Panama	2267	2540	2411	1676	1686	1959	2412

Source: IMF
Note: e estimates

TABLE 11.13   IMPORTS 1980–1986

(US$mn, fob)	1980	1981	1982	1983	1984	1985	1986e
Costa Rica	1375	1091	893	989	1090	1005	1322
El Salvador	897	898	857	892	977	1013	2346
Guatemala	1473	1540	1284	1056	1182	1077	936
Honduras	954	899	681	756	880	954	1106
Mexico	18896	24037	14435	8550	11255	13460	11819
Nicaragua	887	999	775	807	826	836	862
Panama	2995	3316	3045	2321	2503	2712	2955

Source: IMF/national statistics
Note: e estimates

TABLE 11.14   TRADE BALANCE 1980–1986

(US$mn)	1980	1981	1982	1983	1984	1985	1986e
Costa Rica	−374	−88	−23	−107	84	−75	35
El Salvador	177	−100	−158	−157	−251	−304	−496
Guatemala	47	−249	−114	36	−50	−17	14
Honduras	−104	−116	−4	−57	−134	−119	−69
Mexico	−2830	−4099	6795	13762	12941	8407	4664
Nicaragua	−437	−491	−367	−376	−441	−542	−612
Panama	−728	−776	−634	−645	−817	−753	−543

Source: IMF/Euromonitor
Note: e estimates

TABLE 11.15   BALANCE OF PAYMENTS 1980–1985

(US$mn)	1980	1981	1982	1983	1984	1985
Costa Rica	−664	−409	−272	−317	−256	−327
El Salvador	31	−250	−152	−37	−54	n.a.
Guatemala	−163	−573	−399	−224	−377	−246
Honduras	−317	−303	−228	−219	−302	−263
Mexico	−8162	−13899	−6218	5419	4240	540
Nicaragua	−379	−506	−471	−444	462	n.a.
Panama	−311	56	−51	416	99	272

Source: IMF

TABLE 11.16   EXPORTS TO OTHER CENTRAL-AMERICAN COUNTRIES 1985

(US$mn fob) Destination	Costa Rica	El Salvador	Guate-mala	Hon-duras	Mexico	Nicar-agua	Panama
Source:							
Costa Rica	—	49.12	62.7	43.0	13.5	24.7	36.4
El Salvador	25.7	—	111.4	7.5	0.0	4.9	5.0
Guatemala	51.3	161.9	—	54.1	7.3	50.7	15.0
Honduras	7.5	14.4	24.4	—	4.5	9.1	1.7
Mexico	22.0	70.0	94.0	38.0	—	47.0	129.0
Nicaragua	11.6	2.8	11.2	8.2	0.1	—	0.8
Panama	17.7	3.1	2.8	2.3	0.0	1.5	—

Source: IMF

TABLE 11.17   TRADE WITH THE UNITED STATES 1980–1985

(US$mn)	Exports to USA 1980	1983	1985	Imports from USA 1980	1983	1985
Costa Rica	331.4	273.8	441.7	503.8	374.3	430.5
El Salvador	339.8	286.1	375.6	194.2	289.6	490.1
Guatemala	419.9	405.1	407.0	551.8	365.3	445.1
Honduras	437.9	395.5	393.2	426.0	328.5	338.7
Mexico	10072.0	13034.0	15029.0	10890.0	4958.0	11132.0
Nicaragua	160.3	98.6	45.1	242.1	145.1	46.2
Panama	172.6	160.8	289.4	489.1	456.4	544.9

Source: IMF Direction of Trade Statistics

**TABLE 11.18   EXPORTS OF MAJOR COMMODITIES FROM
SELECTED COUNTRIES 1980–1986**

(US$mn)	1980	1981	1982	1983	1984	1985	1986
Coffee							
Costa Rica	247	241	237	230	262	310	219
El Salvador	615	458	406	408	452	453	n.a.
Guatemala	465	296	359	351	366	451	n.a.
Honduras	204	173	153	151	169	185	n.a.
Mexico	444	335	337	513	474	358	374
Nicaragua	166	137	124	150	119	n.a.	n.a.
Petroleum							
Guatemala	n.a.	22	46	60	34	12	n.a.
Mexico	9834	13803	16700	15172	16411	14793	6369
Cotton							
El Salvador	87	55	47	56	10	31	n.a.
Guatemala	166	131	79	46	76	72	n.a.
Mexico	314	302	179	117	208	91	65
Nicaragua	30	123	87	105	134	n.a.	n.a.
Sugar							
Costa Rica	41	43	17	24	32	9	n.a.
Guatemala	69	85	27	127	71	44	52
Honduras	29	47	22	28	26	21	n.a.
Panama	66	53	24	41	33	27	n.a.

Source: Euromonitor/IMF/national statistics

TABLE 11.19   POPULATION 1980–1986

('000s)	1980	1981	1982	1983	1984	1985	1986e
Costa Rica	2250	2270	2320	2440	2420	2600	2720
El Salvador	4510	4590	4660	4720	4780	4820	4960
Guatemala	6920	7110	7320	7520	7740	7960	8050
Honduras	3690	3820	3960	4090	4230	4370	4490
Mexico	69390	71250	73120	74980	76790	78520	80050
Nicaragua	2730	2860	2960	3060	3160	3270	3390
Panama	1900	1940	2040	2090	2130	2180	2225

Source: IMF/World Bank
Note: e estimates

TABLE 11.20   AREA AND POPULATION DENSITY

	Area (sq. km.)	Population density per sq. km. (1985)	Average population growth, 1973–1985
Costa Rica	51000	50.8	2.8
El Salvador	21400	260.0	3.0
Guatemala	108890	73.2	2.8
Honduras	112088	39.0	3.5
Mexico	1958201	40.3	2.8
Nicaragua	147950	22.1	3.1
Panama	77082	28.3	2.3

Source: World Bank

TABLE 11.21   PROJECTED LIFE EXPECTANCY AND TOTAL FERTILITY 1970 AND 1984

	Life expectancy		Total fertility	
	1970	1984	1970	1984
Costa Rica	67	73	5.1	3.3
El Salvador	58	65	6.4	5.3
Guatemala	53	60	6.6	5.8
Honduras	53	61	7.4	6.2
Mexico	61	66	6.6	4.4
Nicaragua	53	60	6.9	5.7
Panama	65	71	5.3	3.3

Source: World Bank

TABLE 11.22   POPULATION STRUCTURE, BY AGE
(Latest official estimates in 1986: percentages of the whole population[1])

	Year	Total	0–14	15–34	35–64	65+
Costa Rica	1984	2415216	34.8	31.2	27.6	6.4
El Salvador	1982	5001000	44.3	——52.1——		3.6
Guatemala	1981	6054227	44.9	32.6	19.4	3.1
Honduras	1981	3820951	47.7	31.6	18.0	2.7
Mexico	1980	67181104	43.0	——52.8——		4.2
Nicaragua	1980	2732520	44.9	30.7	18.3	6.1
Panama	1983	2088585	38.6	35.4	21.4	4.6

Source: Euromonitor, based on UN statistics
Note: [1] Population figures reflect only the results of surveys, and may not correspond exactly with other population statistics give in this section.

TABLE 11.23   RADIO AND TELEVISION STATISTICS 1987
(Estimates based on latest available statistics)

	TV stations	TV sets ('000)	TVs per 1000 inhabitants	Radio channels (approx)	Radio sets ('000)	Radios per 1000 inhabitants
Costa Rica	5	240	92	120	210	81
El Salvador	2	320	68	40	1680	356
Guatemala	5	200	27	85	360	478
Honduras	4	55	13	230	210	51
Mexico	126	12000	160	850	33000	440
Nicaragua	2	200	65	55	850	277
Panama	6	290	139	120	420	201

Source: Euromonitor/statistical offices/UNESCO

TABLE 11.24   SCHOOL ATTENDANCE AND EDUCATIONAL ACHIEVEMENT
(Proportion of the population who have achieved successive stages of state education. Latest available data in 1985)

	Year of survey	Age group surveyed	No education	Did not complete first level	Completed first level	Entered first stage of second level	Entered second stage of second level	Completed third level
Costa Rica	1973	25+	16.1	49.1	17.8	6.3	4.9	5.8
El Salvador	1980	10+	30.2	——60.7——		——6.9——		2.3
Guatemala	1973	25+	93.9	——n.a.——		——4.9——		1.2
Honduras	1983	25+	33.5	——51.3——		4.3	7.6	3.3
Mexico	1980	25+	38.1	31.7	17.3	6.4	1.7	4.9
Nicaragua	1971	25+	53.9	41.8	n.a.	n.a.	4.4	n.a.
Panama	1980	25+	17.4	27.3	23.4	11.7	11.8	8.4

Source: UNESCO

TABLE 11.25   DEVELOPMENT OF THE WORKFORCE 1976–1985

('000s)	1976	1980	1981	1982	1983	1984	1985
Costa Rica	619.5	724.7	726.2	759.9	767.6	839.7	846.8
El Salvador	n.a.	n.a.	n.a.	n.a.	n.a.	n.a.	n.a.
Guatemala	545.6	n.a.	538.7	472.5	n.a.	n.a.	n.a.
Honduras	835.4	966.5	1010.7	1166.5	1210.5	n.a.	n.a.
Mexico	3756.0	5166.0	5825.0	5793.0	5935.0	6429.0	6700.0
Nicaragua	120.9	133.4	n.a.	n.a.	n.a.	n.a.	n.a.
Panama	471.6	n.a.	n.a.	561.1	597.3	613.9	629.6

Source: International Labour Organization

TABLE 11.26   UNEMPLOYMENT 1980–1985

(Euromonitor estimates. Expressed as a percentage of the official workforce. Figures take account of underemployment and under-registration, particularly common in countries marked with an asterisk.)

	1980	1981	1982	1983	1984	1985
Costa Rica	8.0	9.0	10.0	10.0	9.4	11.5
El Salvador*	15.0	20.0	24.0	30,0	30.0	33.0
Guatemala	15.0	16.9	18.0	16.0	17.0	19.0
Honduras	15.0	18.0	21.0	24.0	28.0	34.0
Mexico*	8.0	7.0	15.0	18.5	20.0	18.5
Nicaragua	18.3	14.8	14.5	18.9	21.4	22.2
Panama*	10.0	12.0	14.5	14.0	16.0	17.5

Source: National statistical agencies/Euromonitor

TABLE 11.27   TRANSPORT STATISTICS 1987
(Estimated distances in usable condition)

(km)	Roads	Of which: surfaced	Railways
Costa Rica	22500	6000	1286
El Salvador	16800	9500	602
Guatemala	19500	4750	1828
Honduras	9042	2150	1268
Mexico	217500	117374	27086
Nicaragua	25500	2000	373
Panama	9900	3200	800

Source: National statistical agencies

TABLE 11.28   STRUCTURE OF CENTRAL GOVERNMENT SPENDING 1985

	De-fence	Edu-cation	Health	Housing & social security	Eco-nomic services	Others	Total spending as % of GNP	Surplus/deficit as % of GNP
Costa Rica	3.0	19.4	22.5	17.1	20.2	17.8	24.5	−1.4
El Salvador	20.3	14.5	5.9	3.4	12.6	43.3	19.8	−0.8
Guatemala[1]	11.0	19.4	9.5	10.4	23.8	25.8	9.9	−2.2
Honduras[1]	12.4	22.3	10.2	8.7	28.3	18.1	15.4	−2.7
Mexico	2.7	12.4	1.5	11.9	27.2	44.4	24.9	−7.7
Nicaragua[1]	12.3	16.6	4.0	16.4	27.2	23.4	15.5	−22.2[2]
Panama[1]	0.0	20.7	15.1	10.8	24.2	29.1	27.6	−6.5

Source: World Bank Development Report 1987/national statistical agencies
Note: [1] Figures for 1972
      [2] Figures for 1985

TABLE 11.29   CONSUMER PRICE DEVELOPMENT 1981–1986

(% annual increase)	1981	1982	1983	1984	1985	1986
Costa Rica	37.1	90.1	32.6	12.0	15.0	11.8
El Salvador	14.8	24.7	13.3	11.6	22.3	31.7
Guatemala	9.1	8.7	−2.0	8.4	5.2	31.5
Honduras	9.4	9.0	8.3	4.7	3.3	n.a.
Mexico	27.9	59.0	101.8	65.5	57.8	86.2
Nicaragua	23.9	24.8	31.0	35.4	219.5	n.a.
Panama	7.3	4.3	2.1	1.6	1.0	n.a.

Source: Euromonitor/IMF

TABLE 11.30   FOREIGN DEBT AND EXCHANGE RESERVES 1985

	Total foreign debt (US$ mn)	Foreign exchange reserves (US$ mn)	Gold (troy ounces, Jan 1987)
Costa Rica	4191	506.6	71000
El Salvador	1736	137.7	469000
Guatemala	2595	394.0	522000
Honduras	2713	118.2	160000
Mexico	97429	4906.0	2362000
Nicaragua	5615	391.2	135000
Panama	4020	98.0	n.a.

Source: Euromonitor/IMF/World Bank

TABLE 11.31   STRUCTURE OF THE EXTERNAL DEBT 1970–1985

	Long-term debt (US$ mn)							Short-term debt (US$ mn)	Total external debt (US$ mn) - 1985
	Public and publicly guaranteed		Private non-guaranteed		Use of IMF credit (US$ mn)				
	1970	1985	1970	1985	1970	1985		1985	
Costa Rica	134	3665	112	297	0	189		40	4191
El Salvador	88	1460	88	104	7	89		82	1736
Guatemala	106	2148	14	106	0	116		226	2595
Honduras	95	2178	19	141	0	134		259	2713
Mexico	3196	72510	2770	16500	0	2969		5450	97429
Nicaragua	147	4753	0	0	8	0		862	5615
Panama	194	3276	n.a.	n.a.	0	311		1123	4020

Source: World Bank Development Report 1987

159

TABLE 11.32　BANK LENDING RATES 1980–1986

(average lending rates, %)	1980	1981	1982	1983	1984	1985	1986
Costa Rica	n.a.	n.a.	25.0	23.3	18.0	20.9	21.8
El Salvador	n.a.	n.a.	n.a.	n.a.	n.a.	n.a.	n.a.
Guatemala[1]	8.0	12.0	9.0	9.0	9.0	9.0	9.0
Honduras[1]	16.0	16.0	24.0	24.0	24.0	24.0	24.0
Mexico	28.1	36.6	46.0	63.0	54.7	n.a.	n.a.
Nicaragua	n.a.	n.a.	n.a.	n.a.	n.a.	n.a.	n.a.
Panama	n.a.	n.a.	n.a.	n.a.	n.a.	n.a.	n.a.

Source: IMF
Note: [1] discount rate

TABLE 11.33　US DOLLAR EXCHANGE RATES 1980–1986
(Units of national currency per US dollar, free market rates)

	Unit	1980	1981	1982	1983	1984	1985	1986
Costa Rica	Colón	8.57	21.76	37.41	41.09	44.53	50.45	55.97
El Salvador	Colón	2.50	2.50	2.50	2.50	2.50	2.50	2.50
Guatemala	Quetzal	1.00	1.00	1.00	1.00	1.00	1.00	1.00
Honduras	Lempira	2.00	2.00	2.00	2.00	2.00	2.00	2.00
Mexico	Peso	22.95	24.51	56.40	120.09	167.83	256.87	611.77
Nicaragua	Cordoba	10.05	10.05	10.05	10.05	10.05	26.50	66.50
Panama	Balboa	1.00	1.00	1.00	1.00	1.00	1.00	1.00

Source: IMF

LIST OF TABLES

STATISTICAL FACTFILE

INDEX

(Tables in **Bold**)